BLITZ YOUR LIFE

STORIES FROM AN NFL AND ALS WARRIOR

TIM SHAW

WITH RICHARD SOWIENSKI

DEXTERITY

NASHVILLE

Dexterity, LLC
604 Magnolia Lane
Nashville, TN 37211

First edition: 2017
10 9 8 7 6 5 4 3 2 1

Printed in the United States of America.

ISBN: 978-0-9983253-0-9 (trade paper)
ISBN: 978-0-9983253-1-6 (ebook)

Book design by Grave Distractions Publications.
Cover design by Gore Studio Design.

To all who believe or want to believe that they were made for more.

CONTENTS

FOREWORD

If you know anything about football, you know that a good blitz on the football field isn't a reckless play. It's successful when it is carefully planned, aggressively executed, and perfectly timed. I believe that "blitzing" is the best way to describe how the author, my good friend, has always approached life. To define Tim Shaw as simply a football player or a person battling ALS would fall terribly short of the man I know. Tim is a dreamer, an adventurer, a fierce competitor, a man of faith, and a leader who elevates the people around him. And even in the midst of his fight with a terminal illness, his hope for this book is to help bring out the best in others ... to encourage you to "blitz your life."

I first met Tim the day after I arrived in Nashville from Seattle. We were placed together in a small group of new signees to work out for a couple of days before joining the team. Tim had just been re-signed and was going into his second year in Tennessee. He was a defensive player and special teams star who had the reputation of being a great teammate. As a professional football player, Tim's intensity and work ethic stood out. In the NFL, players are often made team leaders because they are "known" by everyone or they play a high-profile position. I watched how Tim, mainly a special teams player, quickly became a leader in our locker room, not because of status or position, but because of the way he maximized his ability, made the most of every play, and pushed everyone around him to be better. In that 2011 season, Tim was a special teams starter and was voted to be one of the team captains of the Tennessee Titans.

Tim has always been a leader off the field by living what he believes. We spent a lot of time hanging out at team chapels, Bible studies, and service projects. He enjoyed his free time away from football working at church and traveling on mission trips, but even during the season he was out there doing community service work at every opportunity. Tim is one of the most devout followers of Christ that I know, but he isn't a "religious" guy. He wasn't the type of guy to walk around flaunting religious T-shirts or tattoos, and he didn't always feel like he needed to be heard on topics of faith. The way Tim chooses to live every day speaks so much louder than words. At the same time, he has always been ready to talk about his faith when people ask about the source of his contagious view of life.

Tim loves to laugh and have a great time, but he has always looked out for other people. I'll never forget when we were invited to a Keith Urban concert. We were sitting in pretty nice seats, surrounded by people from the country music industry. I'm a fan of all kinds of music but didn't know much about country when I first moved to Nashville. During the concert, Keith Urban took a break from singing and started to talk. I was new to town, had never met Keith, and was confused by his accent, so without thinking I turned to this big group of music people and said, "I didn't know Keith was British?"

Now, Keith Urban is actually from Australia, which is something everybody in Music City knows, especially the folks sitting around us. Before anyone could break the uncomfortable silence and react to my comment, Tim stepped in without skipping a beat and announced loud enough for everyone to hear, "Now, Matt is just making fun of me because I was born in England" (Tim was actually born in Exeter, England). He saved me from looking foolish, but that was typical of Tim—always looking out for the guys around him. While Tim had every intention of making fun of me about it later, he wasn't going to let his quarterback be embarrassed in front of a big group of people. I think anyone who is fortunate enough to be friends with Tim could tell you plenty of stories like that. During my years in Nashville, Tim and I became good friends.

When I received news that Tim was diagnosed with ALS, my wife and I were both devastated. I had played football at Boston College and first learned about ALS because of Pete Frates, a former athlete on the university's baseball team, who had started a campaign to raise money for ALS research called the "Ice Bucket Challenge." But since the first days of the Ice Bucket Challenge, a good family friend of ours had also been diagnosed and eventually lost her life to the unforgiving disease. So I understood the gravity of the diagnosis. I also knew Tim's character and that the disease wasn't going to change his faith or his approach to life. Even still, seeing him out there living life to the fullest and working to help others in the face of the daily challenges that ALS brings has been one of the most inspiring things I have ever witnessed.

I'll never be able to articulate the honor I felt the day Tim called me to ask if I would write the foreword to this book. As we talked, I could hear how the disease had begun to impact his speech, but it was also obvious that ALS hadn't touched Tim's powerful spirit. I knew he was in the middle of a tough day, but he spent the first five minutes of our conversation asking about my family, my life, and just like always, he checked if I was still getting my workouts done. When Tim finally allowed me to ask how he was doing, he explained, "My body is quitting on me. But, Matt, I am doing great—I am learning a lot and really enjoying life." And as we got off the phone that day, Tim did his usual thing. He challenged me to be better, making sure to remind me to do the exercise I had been putting off.

Tim Shaw has always pushed himself to be his best and has focused his energy toward encouraging everyone around him to be better, to love better, and to live better. The Tim I know has always pursued life in an all-out blitz—full of faith, full of passion, and full speed ahead. In the midst of his battle with ALS, he is now challenging you to do the same. I believe Tim's perspectives, his faith, his sense of humor, and the lessons he has poured into this book will inspire you the way it has inspired me. In the following pages, Tim Shaw shares his unique gift for making the world around him a better place—for making us all strive to be the best we can be. You too can learn to Blitz Your Life.

Matt Hasselbeck

Former three-time pro bowl NFL quarterback

ESPN Commentator

INTRODUCTION
Full Speed and Fearless

As long as I can remember, I've loved to run fast.

In high school, I was on the track team and competed in short distance, like the 100-meter and 200-meter races. I still recall those track meets like they were yesterday: the spectators, teammates, and competitors all milling about under the clear blue Michigan skies. I can still see the other runners stretching in the infield, decked out in their colorful school uniforms, with one eye on the events happening all around. Before getting into the blocks, I'd shake my arms and jump up and down a few times to loosen up. Then I would get in position, with the balls of my feet solid against the starting blocks, my fingers digging into the track, anticipating the starting gun…

Bang!

I'd explode out of those blocks, pushing the ground away, creating a wake of wind as I stormed down the track.

In those moments I would experience the feeling, the joy that athletes call being "in the zone." If you've played sports, you know it as the perfect swing of the bat, a three-pointer ripping through the net, or on the football field (the greatest moment of all), flying down the field to make the perfect hit. For my entire life, those brief moments of running *always* brought me a sense of freedom. I lived my life running sure-footed and at full speed.

I suppose that's why it was so strange, then, to have something go wrong while running. I fell during a sprint down the field in a routine kick-off drill at the Tennessee Titans' preseason camp. I had recently experienced some strange twitching and weakness in my right arm and shoulder, but multiple doctors' visits and MRIs had so far been inconclusive. I just assumed it was another nagging injury to tough through.

I was running with the coverage team, weaving around my teammates, when somehow, my foot didn't land correctly. It was a strange sensation, because my foot simply didn't go where my brain told it to go. I stumbled and fell flat on my face. I wasn't tripped or blocked to the ground, and no one else was even close to me.

Of course, I jumped back up as quickly as I could and right back into the action of the drill, knowing that all of my teammates had noticed. And they weren't about to let me off easily.

"Whooo-weee!" one of my buddies called out. "Y'all see the sniper in that tower up there?"

Another guy picked up on the line, "Watch out, fellas! Snipers are out today—they got Shaw."

"Shots fired!" yelled another.

And so it went. There was a lot of laughing and good-natured teasing.

Whatever my teammates thought happened in that moment, they knew tripping over my own feet wasn't typical for me. Flying down the field, *that* was my style of play. Whether as a linebacker or on special teams, I could get to the ball carrier and get there fast. My speed and agility—my ability to run the field—had earned me six years of success in the NFL.

I suppose I had lived my life sprinting in pursuit of one goal after another. I didn't jog through life—I was always running downhill—full speed and fearless was my approach to everything. It didn't make a difference what area of life. If it mattered to me, I went after it like I was sprinting a 100-meter race at a track meet or running down an opposing returner on the football field. Even as I focused on my professional sports career, I still carved out time to earn a master's degree in business at George Washington University while growing a fitness business and launching a real estate company. Anyway you looked at it, on the day of my "mysterious" fall, I was living a life that most folks would call "the dream."

Even though I was in the second year of a three-year contract with the Tennessee Titans, that NFL dream wasn't guaranteed. As they say, NFL also stands for "not for long."

Contract or not, if you're cut, you're out. No team means no pay. The day of my inexplicable fall, I was fighting through my seventh training camp, working to make the 53-man roster.

I finished the practice session strong that day and without further embarrassment. I headed home, feeling confident that my hard work, positive attitude, speed, and skills would once again make me a Titan. As a daily reminder of my monthly and annual goals, I wrote them down on a whiteboard on my bedroom wall. Having a game plan written where I could see it each day was an important habit I had created. I can remember the goals I had on that board like it was yesterday:

- LEAD BY EXAMPLE

- NO MISSED TACKLES

- NO MISSED ASSIGNMENTS

- MAKE THE TEAM

At the end of the long month of Titan's preseason camp in August 2013, just weeks after I had "tripped" while running the kick-coverage drill, life really began to take a turn. I was sitting in the locker room when one of the team scouts hunted me down after practice with the dreaded words, "Coach wants to see you." In the preseason, we called the scout that leads you to the coach's office the "Grim Reaper." I immediately knew my time with the Titans was over. I was led into the office, Coach Mike Munchak nodded to a chair at the conference table, and I sat down. I had great respect for Coach. His office was covered with Titans memorabilia:

plaques, game jerseys, and shelves full of trophies and game balls. All of the things you would expect from the Hall of Fame player.

"I want to thank you for all you've done for the team and organization," Coach Munchak explained. "You've been a big part of the team. I'm sorry it ended this way."

I expressed my appreciation, and we said our goodbyes. Then came the "walk of shame," which required reporting to the general manager, to the trainers to sign releases, and then to the equipment people to check in all my gear. Everything happened so fast that I didn't have time to process it. Within an hour, I was out of there. I left the Titan's facility feeling numb.

In the months after I was cut from the Titans, I worked to get on with another team, but I wasn't picked up. My body kept on struggling, and I knew that if I couldn't train on the level that had kept me in the NFL, I wasn't going to get to play. At some point, I decided I had put my body through enough. I announced my retirement from football in March 2014.

Only a month later, I found myself sitting in another important meeting—this time in a patient examination room at Vanderbilt University Hospital in Nashville. I was waiting to be seen by a neuromuscular specialist, Dr. Donofrio. He had run some tests hours earlier that included an EMG and a nerve conduction study. For the nerve conduction exam, they stuck needles in the different muscles of my arm and leg and sent shocks through the muscles to test the response.

I was pretty confident this meeting would go better than the one with Coach Munchak—I assumed I had a pinched nerve in my neck. Worst-case scenario, I would need an operation to relieve the symptoms. Whatever the doctor had to say, I decided that it couldn't be worse than the message from the scout that had sent me packing.

The doctor finally entered the examination room with one of his assistants. I was sitting in a chair, not on the exam table, having already changed out of the hospital gown. I noticed that he had a piece of paper with about five things scribbled on it. He sat on a little round stool with wheels and rolled closer to me. The assistant stood behind him, close to the door. Dr. Donofrio looked up from the piece of paper he was holding and calmly leveled a diagnosis that would change my life.

"Tim, I believe you have ALS."

My eyes immediately filled with tears as I tried to process what he was saying. He didn't need to explain what ALS meant. Most people think of it as Lou Gehrig's disease. Sports fans can't help but recall the famous scene in *Pride of the Yankees* where Gary Cooper, playing Gehrig, addresses a stadium full of fans, his words echoing through the loudspeaker: "People all say that I've had a bad break. But today ... today, I consider myself the luckiest man on the face of the Earth."

The real Lou Gehrig made that speech in 1939, seventy-five years ago, and not much has changed as far as awareness or treatment of the dreadful disease. ALS (amyotrophic lateral sclerosis) affects the nerve cells of the brain and the spinal cord.

Signals from the brain to the muscles travel over these motor neurons, which in ALS are degenerating and dying. When the signal doesn't get through, voluntary movement and muscle control are lost—which is what happened when I fell during the preseason drill. My brain was telling my foot where to step, but the muscle just didn't get the message.

But Lou Gehrig didn't come to mind in that moment. I was actually thinking of my brother's mother-in-law who had died months earlier from ALS. She went from completely healthy to deceased in less than five years. I could remember her at the end of her battle—consigned to a bed, unable to do anything physically but blink.

As I tried to fight back the tears, the doctor leaned in. "I want you to get a second opinion," he said. "I'm pretty sure, but we want it confirmed."

Dr. Donofrio also wanted me to begin taking a medication called riluzole that had demonstrated some success in slowing the symptoms of the disease. He wanted to know if I had any questions. A million thoughts ran through my head, all of them ending in nightmare scenarios. The only thing I managed to ask him was if I should start taking the drug or wait for a confirming diagnosis.

"Start taking it now," he said.

I tried to hold it together as I left the office. My eyes were watering, but I was still keeping my emotions in check as I waited to get my car from the valet. Once inside my car, I lost it. I began to sob and offer up a jumble of anguished prayers: "Why, God? Why?"

Over the next several weeks, my vision would clear and reality would set in.

I was facing death.

The average lifespan of a person with ALS is two to five years after diagnosis. *Two to five years!*

And even if I beat the odds, how many years could I have? Ten? Fifteen?

It is a ridiculous disease, and it infuriates me that I have so little time left. I have dreams and ambitions, with the whole world in front of me, and now my time is going to be cut short. It isn't right ... it isn't fair.

But then I began to realize I had always been facing death.

We are all going to die.

That's life.

In my case, the experts have just said *when* they think that will happen.

Facing death forces us to analyze what we've done, from the triumphs and joys to the failures and regrets. It makes us answer some tough questions. How have we treated people? Have we accomplished all we wanted? Are we proud of the person we're becoming? It can be difficult to give an honest evaluation, and maybe even more difficult to accept the truth of our lives. Most of us wish we had done things differently, that we were further along toward our goals. Once we are honest with ourselves, it gets even harder, because then we have to act to bring about change.

No wonder facing our mortality is *not* a popular activity.

The doctor's diagnosis snapped this reality into view for me. But I refused to just sit around waiting. I have never lived that way and I never will. I have to live life on my terms, and that means not living afraid of death but pursuing life the way I love to run—an all-out sprint.

So I went to my bedroom and stared at the whiteboard hanging on the wall—the one that held all my dreams and goals. On my whiteboard, in addition to my old football goals, my friend Keith had humorously added a few new items.

He scribbled: "Read more relationship books."

Later he added: "Eat more pizza." And then, "Drink more beer."

I erased all the frivolous and outdated words. I picked up the black marker and filled the board with new goals for the huge challenges I was about to face:

- BE MY TRUE SELF

- IMPACT OTHERS

- LIVE WITH INTEGRITY

- DIE WITH HONOR

My passion hadn't changed, but with one sentence from the doctor, my goals certainly had become much deeper and more meaningful. I realized that I'd been given a gift, a wake-up call that would not allow me to live like I used to live. Along with the ALS diagnosis came the likelihood of a shorter-than-planned future. My "now" was immediately more important because my "later" was in serious jeopardy.

This is life for me today. With my future in doubt, I can't wait, and I can't waste.

Of course, this is the mindset we all should maintain. None of us know when our time is going to be up, but most of us live as if we do. We work for things that don't matter. We have conversations and relationships that are pointless or even harmful. We put off what should be done immediately, because we believe we can do it later. We don't say what we should say now, because we assume we will have another chance. We don't take advantage of today!

It's easy to assume that we will live to see old age. It's normal to operate as if we have nothing but time. We hear and see all the tragedy in the world around us. But instead of admitting the reality that it could have just as easily been us, we operate under the ignorance of thinking, "It won't ever happen to me." The truth is that we are all facing death—with or without a doctor's terminal diagnosis. I believe this understanding should actually free us to live life differently. We should live full speed and fearless, sprinting all-out and in that zone where everything comes together, where we experience a stillness and freedom.

I hate to admit it, but if anyone had ever been prepared to face a terminal illness such as ALS, it was probably me. It's quite unbelievable how I was made ready to battle ALS. To begin with, I was physically prepared to battle the disease. I had an NFL linebacker body with muscles to spare. Since I was also so physically active, I can keep my body working and moving for longer than most people in my situation. From football, I had become not only physically but mentally strong. I need every ounce of mental toughness to attack all that is to come with ALS on a daily basis. This idea first occurred to me while I was standing at the Titans practice facility with dozens of cameras and microphones aimed in my direction. My old team, in my honor, had just completed the ALS Ice Bucket Challenge, a phenomenon that spread across the country in August 2014, bringing awareness to the disease and hope that a cure was possible.

It had been four months since my diagnosis, fractions of the truth were getting out, and I knew I needed to make the news public. The "Ice Bucket Challenge" provided perfect timing for my announcement.

All of a sudden I had a message to share, I still had clear speech to communicate, and I had a platform bigger than anything I could have ever imagined. I was filled with a unique peace and knew I was prepared to face this. Yes, I still struggle every day with the knowledge of the ALS diagnosis, but I'm positive God has made good come from the situation.

Honestly, I wish ALS wasn't part of my story. I think there are many people out there who are living through stories that they wish were not their own. For some reason, this is the story God has given me. Don't get me wrong—I'm not some perfect guy. I am definitely no saint or preacher. I still go through cycles of anger and questioning and sadness. Even as I write this today, my body is deteriorating at an unbelievable rate. Muscle fiber by muscle fiber is quitting despite all of my efforts, prayers, and desperate pleas for God's mercy. But I feel an urgency to use the time I have left to tell my story. I feel a calling to share some of the particulars of my struggle with ALS, some of the lessons of my journey, and some of the amazing people I have come to know who are living lives that inspire me to keep sprinting toward my goals. My hope is that this book and these stories will help encourage you to "blitz your life": to go all-out in pursuing your passion *now*, embracing your unique gifts and talents, fearlessly facing the challenges on the road ahead, and becoming your best self.

EMBRACE
YOUR CRAZY

1
CRAZY LOVE

I'm a hitman. That's what I would tell people who asked me what I did for a living. I hit people. Some might call that crazy. But I don't think that qualifies me as crazy—as a linebacker and a special teams monster, my job was to stop the guy with the football, which meant knocking him to the ground.

You know what was crazy?

The pure joy I experienced in my heart while hitting people!

In fact, when I think about that joy, I think about a perfect hit. One of those perfect hits came against the Philadelphia Eagles when I was playing for the Chicago Bears in 2009.

It was a Sunday night game in November, and the weather was great for players: below 50 degrees but still above freezing. Cool enough for a sweat to feel good but not enough to be cold. In anticipation of the kickoff, more than seventy thousand screaming fans rose to their feet. I was behind and to the left of the kicker, aligned on the field's painted numbers. I keyed on the kicker, knowing his exact step that would signal me to take off and hit the line of scrimmage running at full speed. The booted ball soared high into the air. Most NFL kickers can boot the ball at least sixty-five yards. Our kicker, Robbie Gould, would typically give me a perfectly placed shot, knocking the ball a couple yards deep into the end zone with an incredible hang time of four-plus seconds. That meant, as a former high school sprinter, I could cover a lot of the football field while the ball was still in the air.

Robbie kicked it to number 35, Eagles return man Macho Harris. He caught it on the goal line and headed up field. The return was designed to hit straight up the middle of the field, but a Bears teammate on the outside funneled him back toward me. In the meantime, I was rocketing down the turf. I could see the whole field in front of me: their blockers, my teammates, the runner and his likely path up the field. I adjusted my angle, beating an Eagles blocker. The Eagles were trying to protect Harris with a two-man wedge, but they were not looking at me, they were looking to block one of my teammates. Big mistake, because it gave me a clear shot at Macho just five yards in front of me. I launched with all my might toward him, a 238-pound missile fueled by adrenaline. I couldn't hear the crowd yelling. I didn't see my teammates. I didn't see Harris's blockers. I didn't see anything except Harris right in front of me with his green and silver helmet lowered. All the hard work. All the training. For the anticipation of this moment.

Crack!

The sound of pad exploding on pad filled the stadium. I hit him at just the right angle, and Harris was lifted off his feet and pancaked onto his back with an *umphff*. The hit was so pure I didn't even feel it. I sprung up from the turf and jumped up and down, slapping my helmet like a crazed gorilla. The crowd roared their approval and the fans were high-fiving each other as my teammates joined my celebration. If you could've seen my face, I'm sure you would have recognized the same kind of joy as a kid getting a new bike at Christmas, an A+ on a final exam, or even a first kiss from a first love. To get that kind of joy from knocking down a guy carrying this funny-shaped leather ball, now *that's* crazy. And I love it.

The Right Amount of Crazy

From the first time I got to play football in helmet and pads, I loved the contact, the pure physicality of it. I had the perfect amount of crazy—not enough to be reckless and get hurt, but enough to let go of reservations and hesitations and play the game all out.

I blame (or thank) my dad for this craziness. My father, a teacher and elementary school librarian, is the most adventurous person I know. After graduating from Cambridge (he's from England), he moved to Africa and lived with missionaries. As part of the VSO (Voluntary

Services Overseas—the English equivalent of the Peace Corps), he taught English. When it was time to return home to England, at the age of twenty, he decided to take the slow route home. He and his two sisters, along with three friends, hitchhiked across the Sahara Desert. From Ayangba, Nigeria, through Agadez, Niger, to Algiers, Algeria, we're talking 2,600 miles—and as you may know, it's the hottest place on the planet, with average highs over 100 degrees.

Hitchhiking, Dad explained, was a bit different over there. Truck drivers would often supplement their incomes by letting people ride along for a fee, though signs would be posted saying in French, "Passengers Forbidden." You might have fifty people hanging on the sides or huddled in the back of a semi-trailer truck. At night, Dad and his group would sleep on the sand in front of the parked truck so when the driver started it in the morning they would hear it. Getting left behind in the middle of the desert would not have been a good thing!

Maybe his desert experience helps explain his love, his need, to head for the water whenever he can. Growing up, we would vacation every summer in Marquette, in Michigan's Upper Peninsula, a seven-hour drive from my hometown of Livonia, Michigan. As we drove by Lake Michigan, if there were white caps on the lake, we would have to stop and catch a few waves whether the sun was shining at 2 p.m. or the moon was shining at 2 a.m.

Then, during our vacations in Marquette, we progressed to jumping off cliffs into the water below. Black Rocks provided great thrills. So did Presque Isle and Stoney Mills.

But it wasn't only "going down"—cannonballing off cliffs a couple stories high into the lake below—that got my crazy going. There was also a bit of craziness "going up." Let me explain.

During the summers, my parents worked at a Bible camp, so my brothers and I became "camp brats," not only helping with the kids and chores, but also exploring everything surrounding the camp. Across the lake from the camp, we could see a massive radio tower rising into the air. We found out it was 355 feet tall. That's 55 feet taller than a football field! It would be like standing on a bit of metal scaffolding thirty-two stories high. Just my kind of craziness. So at sixteen, in the dead of night, a friend and I snuck out to climb the tower. I counted every rung to the top. At the top, the only illumination was the blinking red light warning pilots to keep their distance. Thinking I'd reached the goal, my friend told me that it didn't count until I touched the red light, another 12 feet up a narrow mast. So I climbed up and kissed the light!

Of course I'm not suggesting this is what you should do. This is my particular brand of crazy. Eventually the daredevil climbing turned into violent athletic explosions at precise moments.

Is there risk in letting your crazy out?

Yes.

Am I challenging people to take dangerous risks or have the guts to do wild things?

No. Not unless you're called to extreme sports or other physically demanding, fear-conquering professions.

But I am suggesting that you eliminate the "I can'ts" and "I shouldn'ts" from your vocabulary. I'm talking about the crazy it takes to pursue a passion when it's against all odds, to stand out and excel.

Crazy Dive

Another high climber—and high diver—who wouldn't take no for an answer was Katura Horton-Perinchief. I first met Katura at George Washington University when we were studying for our MBA degrees. Born in Bermuda, Katura said she had been diving off boats since age two and fell in love with diving when she was five. From that age forward, Katura said she wanted to be an Olympian.

"The island boasts beautiful, clear blue waters and pink sandy beaches along with plenty of places for a young adrenaline junkie to get her fix of diving off high things," Katura said.

But her diving career really took off when her family moved to Toronto while her mother attended school. In Toronto, her mother signed her up for diving lessons, as well as gymnastics, swimming, and skating. But it was diving where she found her calling. When she was eight, she started platform diving—that means diving from a board about as tall as a three-story building! At age nine, she was the youngest ever Provincial champion. She was Canadian Age Group champion at fifteen, winning the one-meter springboard, three-meter springboard, and platform events. She went on to represent Canada at international meets for the next three years.

When it came time to choose a college, Bermuda was out of the question because they only had two-year programs equivalent to our community colleges in the United States. Katura decided to call the coach at the University of Texas, which had the top diving program in the country. Better yet, Texas's coach was also the US Olympics coach. Although she had full scholarship offers elsewhere, because of the incredible program, Katura went to Texas on a partially funded academic scholarship. Once at UT, she quickly earned an athletic scholarship as well and ultimately earned All-Big 12 Conference honors.

Through all of her training, she did have to push back on naysayers. Katura said some well-meaning people tried to push her in a different direction, pointing out that she might be better suited for swimming or volleyball. They said she was too tall (in college she stood five-foot-six, about the average height of a male diver) and that she had the wrong body type.

"All the morning and evening practices, all the muscle aches and pains, it all paid off on August 22, 2004, when I stepped onto the three-meter springboard at the Olympics in Athens," Katura said. Not only did she become Bermuda's first female diver, she also became the first black female diver—from any country—in Olympic history.

Today she's introducing young Bermudians to diving, serving on the Bermuda Olympic Association, and using her masters of public health to track cancers on the island as manager of the Bermuda National Tumour Registry.

Yes, jumping off a three-story-high platform is crazy. ("Any little error hurts," Katura reminded me.) Following your dream to be an Olympian—crazy. Becoming the first black female diver in Olympic history—crazy. That's what it means to embrace your crazy.

Of course, crazy comes in all different sizes.

Crack House Crazy

As another great example of crazy, I have to tell you about Dr. Howard Olds and Courtney and Brian Hicks. They spearheaded a nonprofit in Nashville called Harvest Hands. Brian, the executive director of Harvest Hands, recounted how the organization got started. "In 2007, we began a ministry called Harvest Hands. The birth of Harvest Hands was shaped by the belief that God calls us to do things that sometimes appear crazy to others."

Dr. Olds was senior pastor at Brentwood United Methodist Church and mentor to Brian. Dr. Olds led a group of members from his suburban church to a high-crime area south of downtown Nashville where a neighborhood meeting was going on. At the meeting, Dr. Olds asked a simple question: Would the community be open to a new ministry in their neighborhood committed to working with them to make a positive impact and to be good neighbors?

"One man at the meeting," Brian recalls, "stood up and said, 'This all sounds good, but other groups have come and said similar stuff before. We'll believe it when we see it.' The neighbors were skeptical for good reason—too often people don't do what they say they're going to do."

Dr. Olds asked where they would like them to begin.

"'If you really want to do something,' the neighbor replied, 'do something about the crack house at the top of the hill.'"

What the people in the neighborhood didn't know was that Dr. Olds was dying of cancer. "He was at a place in his life where he was committed to living like he was dying," Brian said. "He was bold, and he was not afraid to take risks."

He went back to his church and said, "We're buying a crack house in South Nashville."

Imagine the response of the board of trustees. Some folks expressed serious doubts: it wasn't safe; they needed to be careful; it wasn't a "good investment." But Dr. Olds and his team of leaders were convinced of God calling them to do something crazy to reach the community, so they started negotiations to buy the run-down crack house and its adjoining lot. After contacting the owner, they settled on a price of $300,000, two or three times what it was worth. The week after closing the sale, they tore it down and began to build Harvest Hands on that same lot.

Their decision has had a lasting impact on the community and continues to bring new life to children and families in the area. Harvest Hands provides with their after-school tutoring programs for kids of all ages and teaches life and business skills through their soap-making and coffee-roasting businesses. The area has seen great improvements with new restaurants, businesses, and homes. In fact, it's become so successful that Brian and his team now have their sights set on another neighborhood, south and east of downtown Nashville—the most dangerous, high-crime neighborhood in the city. How dangerous? They bought a warehouse and refurbished it to accommodate more classrooms, meeting areas, and a retail store for their handmade soaps and specialty coffee roasts. During construction, Brian explained that he received calls from these big, burly construction workers who were worried about their own safety. They told Brian it wasn't safe in that neighborhood. "Exactly!" Brian said. "That's why we're going there."

That's the kind of crazy that can change a neighborhood and a city.

Janitor at the Grammys Crazy

I've had the great fortune of meeting amazing people who have become important in my life. One such person is Morris Chapman.

I met Morris through my friend Tim who visited Saddleback Church—the megachurch pastored by Rick Warren—in California. Leading the music that day was guest worship leader Morris Chapman. After the service, my friend and Morris talked. They became friends and stayed in touch. At one point, Tim told Morris about me. This was in 2011, before my ALS diagnosis. For some reason, Morris wanted to talk to me. He called me a couple times, but I didn't get around to calling him back until I was at the Milwaukee airport. I'm glad I took the time to call, because we had this instant connection. He had this ability to say the right words of encouragement and to remind me that I was loved; he lifted my spirits. When Morris was scheduled to visit a church near Nashville, I invited him to stay with me. Morris, I learned, had a remarkable story.

Born in 1938 in Central Arkansas, Morris grew up experiencing racism. Hoping for better job opportunities, he and his family moved to Las Vegas. Morris was nineteen years old at the time. But even there, in spite of better-paying jobs, color made a difference. Blacks could only enter the hotels and casinos through the back door. In fact, even entertainers of color couldn't stay in the hotels where they were entertaining, including Pearl Bailey, Nat King Cole, Fats Domino, and Sammy Davis Jr. They were put up in small cottages behind the hotel properties, or they were bussed to boarding houses in the black neighborhoods.

Morris ended up taking a job as a janitor in the Las Vegas school district. Although he had never had piano lessons and couldn't read music, he had a great ear—a gift and passion to play piano and sing. During breaks at school, he would often play in the music room. On weekends, he would lead worship services at different churches throughout Las Vegas.

Morris continued working as a janitor during the week and leading worship services and speaking to groups part time. One day, he was at a businessmen's breakfast meeting and he told a joke that led to a life-changing decision. He recounted the story in his autobiography, *I Know the Plans*:

"A man had ... fallen over a cliff, as he tumbled down the cliff, he grabbed a bush, held on, and cried out for help. Jesus came to the edge of the cliff and said, 'If you will let go of the bush, I will catch you.' The frightened man felt his fingers slipping further down the bush. Finally, he hollered at Jesus, 'Hey, anyone else up there?'"

Morris explained after telling the joke, he believed God was telling him to let go. So at the age of forty, he let go of the safe, comfortable life and "embraced his crazy" by going into full-time music ministry.

Soon after making that decision, Morris came to Nashville and recorded an album produced by the legendary (and eccentric) Gary S. Paxton. That opened doors, said Morris, and he went on to lead worship services throughout the country. He wrote and recorded several more albums and was nominated for a Grammy and three Dove awards. Fifteen years after entering the music worship scene full time, he was playing at conventions in Las Vegas in the rooms that he had once been blocked from entering. This, from a man who had dropped out of high school and flunked English class![1]

As you can see, crazy is a mindset.

Crazy is the ability to let go of all outside forces and influences.

So what's your crazy? What is the crazy that allows you to stare fear and doubt right in the face? A kind of crazy that can lead to accomplishments, from individual success in athletics to success in remaking a neighborhood to success in bringing joy and hope through music to hundreds of thousands of worshippers nationwide.

Write Down Your Crazy!

Before I began writing down my goals on a whiteboard, I wrote them down in notebooks or journals. I was going through a box of my old journals—I guess I'm sort of a pack rat—and came across a notebook page with the goals I had written down after being drafted by my first team, the Carolina Panthers. Here were some of my top goals:

- Seek God Today

- Make This Team

- Lead Special Teams In Tackles

- All-Rookie Team

I made the team and led the special teams in tackles. And I was on my way to being the leading tackler on special teams for the Bears and Titans later in my career. It began with clear goals set down in writing. Without clear goals, your life is a ship without a rudder. If you don't know where you want to go, you'll never get there.

Not surprisingly, there have been studies that support the idea that putting your goals in writing will lead to a higher level of achievement. A couple of researchers from Dominican University, in River Forest, Illinois, conducted a study on writing down short-term goals. In the study, participants were randomly assigned to five different groups:

1. Unwritten Goals.

2. Written Goals.

3. Written Goals and Action Plan.

4. Written Goals, Action Plan, and Tell a Friend.

5. Written Goals, Action Plan, Tell a Friend, and Report Progress.

The Group 1 people were asked to simply think about their goals, what they wanted to accomplish over the next four weeks. Group 2 was asked to write down their goals. In addition to that, Group 3 had to come up with an action plan, or as the study called it, "action commitments." Group 4 would go further by telling a supportive friend about the goals and the action plan. Finally, Group 5 was also going to give weekly updates on their progress to the friend.

After the study was finished, here's the bottom line according to the researchers: "Those who wrote their goals accomplished significantly more than those who did not write their goals." Telling a friend about their goals and updating them on progress also led to significantly more accomplishments.[2]

The research backs up what I've known from my own personal experience and probably what your common sense tells you as well. Do you want to increase your chances to accomplish something?

Write it down!

That's right, write down your crazy!

Put it where you will see it often, reminding you what you're working toward.

And to be clear, not all success needs to be measured in money. Often, money and success do go hand in hand, but it doesn't need to. For some, like Brian with Harvest Hands or Morris with his music ministry, success can be measured by lives touched, by lives put right, by lives given a chance for a better future. Morris, for example, never even asked for a set fee for his concert tours to churches and organizations. He asked for a "free will" or "love offering" from the people he ministered to. In other words, the organizers "passed the hat" and people gave whatever they felt like giving. Sometimes the collection was quite adequate and at other times painfully small. But Morris knew he was doing something important, that he was fulfilling his dream.

Whiteboard Goals: Seize the Marker

Yes, it's crazy to dream big and even crazier to tell people about your dreams. It takes some work for you to let go and let your crazy out—but it all begins when you write it down. At the end of every chapter, I'm going to suggest that you commit to writing something about your future plans. Make your goals real by writing them down. Don't simply think about it. Get out pen and paper or create a new file on your computer or—like me—get a whiteboard.

Carpe marker! Seize the marker and write down your crazy dream.

2
WHO ARE YOU?

The boat chugged southeasterly down the wide, brown Amazon River. A group of lay volunteers (myself included) and missionaries had just left Manaus, Brazil, the capital of the state of Amazonas, for the twenty-hour trip to Maués, a town of about 22,000 with another 20,000 inhabitants spread along 140 river villages.

From Maués, our band of twenty-six crammed onto a smaller boat—more like a commercial trawler than a passenger ship—and traveled another five hours to the village where we would build a well, giving its people access, for the first time, to clean water.

I had been on mission trips before to Costa Rica and Haiti, but this was my first trip to Brazil. I was intrigued by this trip because I was told it was in the middle of nowhere and we would work hard, which is what I wanted. We would provide assistance that would make an immediate impact on the lives of those we were serving. The villagers had, up to this point, bathed, cooked, and drank from the same river water. Clean water would greatly reduce sickness. In addition to helping others, I enjoyed deepening current friendships and developing new ones on these adventures. Finally, I knew that one way or another, as on past mission trips, I would receive something more than what I gave. That certainly turned out to be the case this time.

Arriving at the village, we tied up to the bank. The homes were pieced together, it seemed, with any material available, from corrugated tin to concrete blocks to thatch. They lined the river and were also set back into the jungle. After disembarking, Marquinhos, the missionary leader of our group, introduced us to the local pastor and a number of villagers. We unloaded supplies and got right to work. Days were spent hauling tools and pipe up to the high point where the drilling—mostly by hand—was going on. In the evening we would return to the boat. We would clean up, eat dinner, and hang our hammocks in preparation for the night's sleep. Then, in the pitch dark, we would head to church, flashlights in hand. By the time our group arrived, the village congregation would already be rocking and rolling.

The church, as you might expect, was a simple structure. A cement slab. Long wooden benches. Posts, no walls, holding up a tin roof. A generator powered a few bare light bulbs, an amplifier, and a guitar.

In spite of the primitive conditions, it was the most carefree, charismatic church service I'd ever attended. I say carefree, but to my tame American sensibilities, it sometimes seemed more like chaos. There was lots of hand clapping, shouts of praise, and loud singing to accompany the guitar, which was played with more enthusiasm than skill. Kids were running in and out of the wall-less building, and mothers unabashedly breastfed their babies. Insects buzzed and battered the bare bulbs, and I sat on a bench drenched in sweat, soaking in the humid and joyful atmosphere. The singing, praying, and preaching was in Satere, the local Portuguese dialect, leaving me to supply my own words, to look within myself, and to open my heart to God.

One night, in the midst of this jubilant worship service, I was sitting on the bench with my eyes closed, praying. Marquinhos, as a guest pastor, was preaching to the boisterous congregation, when I felt hands lifting me upward. Marquinhos was waving me forward. He knew I was struggling physically, even though I didn't yet know what was wrong. Someone in the crowd translated, "They want to pray for you."

I was herded to the front of the church and then surrounded by the congregation. I had been "prayed over" before, but nothing like this. Hands were being placed all over my body as they prayed. I could distinguish about twenty voices and three or four languages. I didn't specifically know what was being said, but I knew it was being said fervently.

What I felt was a pouring out of love and care. Marquinhos was praying for the healing of my body. How could this man who had known me for less than a week care for me this much, to be so moved and heartbroken over my situation? Marcos, a missionary traveling with us from Maués, along with his twelve-year-old daughter Kaykay, were pleading with God on my behalf. Here were people I barely knew, some of whom I would never see again after I left, pouring their hearts out for me.

As they prayed, tears streamed down my face. I felt a deep peace settle in, and I knew that I was exactly where I was supposed to be. I have talked about when an athlete, through training and preparation, can sometimes feel like he or she is "in the zone," where the rim seems as big as a hula hoop, a baseball as slow and big as a softball, a hit so pure on a ball carrier it's like landing on a cloud. I was in a spiritual zone, feeling love like I had never felt love before. A feeling—more than a feeling, a certainty—that God was in this place and He was in control. It was more than a rush of endorphins, more than intellectual acceptance of someone's concern for my well-being. Though words can never adequately describe the experience, it was nothing short of an encounter with God, as real as the water flowing from our newly dug well.

When the praying ended, I returned to my bench changed, fortified, emboldened, assured.

At the end of the week, with our work completed, I returned to the States with the memory of this experience branded deep within.

I Am Not Football

A month after returning from Brazil, I received the ALS diagnosis. Not only had my football career ended, but now I also had to deal with ALS. First, fear settled in. Because of my faith in God, I knew it wasn't the fear of death, but it took me a while to pinpoint exactly what it was that I feared. Sure, I was afraid of the highly probable process of losing all my physical functions, slowly becoming more and more disabled, my fully functional mind trapped in an unresponsive body. But it was more than the debilitating progression of the disease that caused me to fear.

Over time, I realized that it was the remainder of my life that I actually feared. More specifically, everything that I would do or not do from this point onward, until the Grim Reaper came for me, would have magnified significance.

Every choice.

Every action.

Every word.

I was afraid of not making the most of whatever time I had. I was afraid of dying with a feeling of "I should have done more," that my life was cut short before I accomplished what I was *meant* to do.

Once I was able to identify it, I still didn't know what to do about the fear. My initial reaction was to ignore it and carry on with normal life as best I could. It wasn't denial; it was just that I was already doing the things I wanted to do. People assumed I was bucket-listing, but I wasn't doing that at all. I was just living life on my terms, I thought, like I always had.

A change was in order, but how? Did I give up the life I loved and had worked hard for? How I changed, to some extent, was up to me, but with consent or not, change, "it was a-coming." I'd rather have a little control, so I had to figure out how to do it. I had to take a look at my life as it was now, but also from the perspective of where I had been.

From age twelve to twenty-nine, football was my life. Really, from age fourteen on, everything I did revolved around the game. I got good grades and stayed out of trouble so I could play football. My schedule was dictated by games, practices, and rest. All for the game. Even while playing other sports, football ruled. I played basketball to improve lateral quickness and hand-eye coordination. I ran track to improve straight-line speed for football. It's a wonder I didn't run the one 100-meter dash with a football tucked under my arm. During basketball season I would brick a free throw and my coach would ask, "Tee, you been lifting weights?"

"Nah, Coach," I'd say with a smirk. We both knew I had.

In college it became even worse. I wanted to become a superstar. The game consumed my every thought. The next day's workout dictated when I would eat and sleep. Life was all about what was happening in my football world.

The pros took it to the highest level. Nothing else mattered. The team basically owned us, and that was fine because they wrote the big checks. Every conversation, it seemed, centered on the game. I'm not complaining. I loved it. But really, looking back, I see there was a problem.

The problem was I believed I *was* football. That's who I was. The most important thing about me. It's what defined me. How could I possibly think otherwise? It was in *everything* I did. Even if I tried to get away from it, somehow it showed up. Anywhere I went, someone would ask about it. The game brought me opportunities, fortune, and fame. It led me to relationships and a life I only once dreamed of.

But football wasn't who I was, just like your job isn't who you are. Football was what I did for a long time. It was my main avenue of expressing myself. It was where I felt most comfortable and fulfilled. But it wasn't who I was. I had to learn that my identity was not football. If football was my identity, then when football came crashing down (and it did), my life would crash as well. If my identity was wrapped up in such an unpredictable, unreliable thing as football, then I was setting myself up for confusion and deep loss. If all of who I am depends on someone else's approval (a coach) and the success of a project (winning a game), then my life will be a roller coaster of highs and lows as my identity is tossed around, out of my control.

My friend Dave Ball, at the end of his NFL career, found himself facing the same doubts and confusion. Dave played defensive end for UCLA, where he held the record for quarterback sacks and in 2003 was named PAC 10 Defensive Player of the Year. He was drafted by the San Diego Chargers and went on to play for the New York Jets and the Carolina Panthers, who cut him in September of the 2007 season.

Talented players can find themselves without a team for any number of reasons: too many players at one position, coaching changes, a defensive coach that prefers speed over size, or vice versa. To the player cut, the reason doesn't matter.

When Dave was cut, he and his wife and their one-year old son had to move back home with Dave's parents, in the house he grew up in. "I felt like a failure," Dave said. "I felt like a dirtbag every day."

After the 2007 season, Dave was picked up by the Tennessee Titans, and he played for another five years before retiring.

"When I was done with football," he said, "everything was stripped away from who I thought I was. That was extremely painful."

Dave said that his focus on football prevented him from looking at areas of his life that needed to be addressed. "It was a Band-Aid over my life. Now all the Band-Aids were getting torn off," he explained.

He said the hardest lesson he learned is that what this world tells you to be is not who you should be. For example, he said that as a boy you're told that if you're an athlete, if you're physically talented, you're *better* than others. If you make a lot of money, you're better than others. If you can influence women—be with a lot of women—you're better.

"That's what I was brainwashed with. Even though I've always been humble and self-critical," he said, "deep down I believed these things."

Dave said he came to realize that football was the ultimate false validation of who he was, and so he set out to find out who he truly was.

I Am Not ALS

I'll never forget running into someone at the pool shortly after I went public with my diagnosis. He recognized me: "You're the ALS guy!" But just as I am not "Tim the Football guy," I am not "Tim the ALS guy."

ALS doesn't define me. ALS sucks. It's the most physically and mentally difficult thing I have ever had to endure. In my current state, I have to think about every move I make. Literally, every time I move. Sit down. Stand up. Turn the corner. Walk through a doorway. Navigate through a crowd. If I'm not careful, I will fall. I'll run into something or someone. My body doesn't do what I tell it to, and my balance resembles that of a newborn calf.

So if I'm not the football guy or the ALS guy, who am I?

I had to start with self-evaluation. I know this is what Dave Ball went through, and I believe a lot of people can relate to finding themselves in a time of change, whether it's a new career or opportunity or a position where change is necessary. Situations like these require honest introspection. For me, that meant analyzing my priorities. Do I work on my golf handicap, pursue business ventures, read a good book? These are all things I love to do and there is nothing wrong with any of them, but isn't there something more meaningful? I guess that depends on what I really want to accomplish. How about peace on earth, or at least *inner* peace? Now, I didn't want to spend the rest of my time meditating. My thirty-year-old self hadn't thought about all that serious stuff. But like me (even if it's not life or death), a lot of us need to face this fear and answer the question:

If you could have, do, be, go, or experience *anything* at all, what would that be?

Most people never answer such introspective questions. If not for ALS, I don't know when I would have faced this daunting question. I decided that in order for me to live fully, I needed to run this question down and face it head-on.

Surprisingly, my answer wasn't very difficult to find. What I wanted more than anything else was *impact*. I believe that as humans our time on earth is short, so the greatest thing I can ever do is to positively impact as many people as I possibly can. I've had some cool experiences, and I'll have some more as I go along. I've made money and had fun, but if I died tomorrow, I would have wanted to leave a positive impact on other people.

Knowing what I really want, having answered that question, I realized I must act on this grand self-discovery immediately. For me, this action has taken many forms. Some are small and short term, like doing an interview for a local paper or speaking at or supporting charity events. Others are larger and hopefully will have a longer lasting impact. Like this book, for instance. My hope is that something in it will lift somebody today and for who knows how many years after I'm long forgotten. I've also looked for ways to team up with others who want to make a lasting difference. Along those lines, my friends Tom and Stacey and I formed a sports performance company that we hope will bring character and leadership development to young people through sports while promoting diversity and merging cultures.

These are the types of things that I believe can have lasting impact and change lives.

I haven't quit golfing or traveling or having fun. Those things are important too, as they fuel my spirit, but now they are prioritized in their proper place. I've adjusted other things as well to reflect my new goals. It's not like I dropped everything in pursuit of my drive to impact other people in a positive way, but I did sharpen my focus. Spending time with family is important to me, so I've made seeing them frequently a huge priority.

I also make a lot of choices to *not* do things that I don't want to do. I know I, like so many people, used to do many things I didn't actually want to do—either out of a sense of obligation, pity, or even guilt. I simply don't do that anymore. And I am free not to do these activities because I have faced and answered the question of what I really want. If something asked of me doesn't align with my priorities, then I simply don't do it. Below the surface of this seemingly selfish approach is one of genuine care for others. This methodology doesn't negate charity or helping others, but it eliminates the *obligation* to do anything. If, by your choice, you leave your path to do something out of your purpose, then that's awesome. But giving your precious time by any means other than your own choice doesn't benefit anyone. Breakfast with a long-lost third cousin stopping through town? Sure, if you want to. Giving the keynote speech at a fundraising event? Not if done solely out of guilt. Getting coffee with someone who drains you? No, you don't have to. That phone call with an ex? Heck no, that's just a huge waste. Big or small, there's rarely anything wrong with these activities. What matters most is *why* we choose to do them. Knowing what you really want allows you the freedom to make those choices.

Dave, after his football career, sought counseling and in the process developed a strong sense of purpose for his life.

"I believe I was put here to build and be in loving relationships with people, and I was put here to help serve others," he said.

Today Dave is helping college coaches find out what's going on under the surface of their teams and turn struggles into success. He also serves on the Williamson County Foster Care Review Board and the Nashville Coaching Coalition.

"I am an extremely passionate man who is trying to be a great dad, a great husband, and do something of value," he said.

Who Are You?

Take a step back to evaluate who you are. What are your core beliefs and values, your belief system? The way we handle success and failure shows what we truly believe. Our actions—not our words—display what we truly believe.

Look at the small decisions you make. Who are you influenced by? What do you agree or disagree with? Where do you draw the line? Do you place high value on personal success and public recognition? Or do you quietly accept success, acknowledging team efforts? When you fail, do you beat yourself up and not forgive yourself?

These questions can help define who you are as a person.

Sometimes we are blind to our own beliefs. We deny that certain actions reveal certain beliefs. If you constantly put your needs ahead of everyone else's—like a guy I know (*cough, Tim Shaw*)—then you are showing a belief that you are more important than those around you. Even if you never admit it, your actions demonstrate it clearly. We are often unaware of the statements that our actions are making. If the things that I claim to believe don't come out in my actions at all, do I really believe those things? I might wish I had a high moral standard, but if I'm constantly doing morally questionable things, then the reality is that I don't have high moral standards. The truth is revealed in our actions, particularly when moments of pressure reveal what lies beneath our conscious motivations.

For example, while I am quick to forgive a family member, I tend to be harsh with other people, projecting my own expectations and standards onto them. If I'm not cutting other people slack, then I'm not showing the kind of grace that I want to be one of my core beliefs. My actions say otherwise.

On a more positive note, during a football game, in the heat of the moment so many actions are reactions. I have been hit after a play had ended, and I immediately confronted the guilty party. I did not retaliate, but I made sure it was clear that such actions were not cool. I always stood my ground and made sure that I won my battles between the whistles, which was the ultimate reward. My reaction could have easily been one of retaliation, which would have vindicated me at the expense of my team. My value of "team above self" trumped my desire for revenge and dictated my actions. When we react and do not have time to think, that's when our true values show up. We can't draft a response or take time to decide how to react, it just happens. And when desired values become automatic reactions, we know they have become part of who we are.

Wrestling with values and beliefs can be a struggle, especially when there is a gap between who you want to be and who you are now. The beliefs and values that you strive toward are not always easily attained. You may not immediately succeed at being the person you want to be, but failure is part of the process. In fact, failures can become great learning experiences that propel you toward who you want to become. It may take many failed attempts to see the values become your own, but failure can indicate progress if followed up by corrective action.

In the process of discovering your core beliefs, you are also discovering who you truly are. As you develop a belief system to live by, your true self shows more and more. This does not mean you are a finished product, but it does mean you are a work in progress, and committing to the process is half the battle. As your belief system grows and changes, you will grow and change. As life continues to throw its experiences at you, your core beliefs will continue to be challenged. Day in and day out, people will question who you are and what you are doing. Without strong convictions, you will be easily swayed. The more you know yourself, the more you can stand firm in your beliefs and your actions.

Whiteboard Goals: I Am...

If you are *not* your job, who are you? If you are *not* the latest fashion trend, who are you? This chapter's whiteboard goals assignment calls for you to take a few minutes to think about who you are and what you value. Is it, for example, independence, lots of human interaction, teamwork, hard work, creativity, or service to others? Write down the core beliefs you think define you. Or write about the times you have failed and how that made you a better person. If you want to write a bit more, consider if you have ever had a "mountaintop" experience. Though it might be difficult to describe, what insights did you gain about yourself?

3
A Shoe of a Different Color

As a six-year-old, I walked into first grade with two different shoes on. Not by accident. Not just one day. Pretty much the whole year. I had my Elmer Fudd hat and flannel shirt that I loved, and then I had my shoes to make me different. As a first-grader, I wasn't making a statement, I simply liked the idea of wearing two different shoes—it was a confident and unconscious expression of creativity.

In second grade, I stood on the big stage and screamed out my auditioning lines for the school musical. That self-confidence was met with smirks and ridicule. I learned that other kids had their own opinions about what was acceptable. This realization made me feel self-conscious, though I continued to feel confident in my own abilities.

I wouldn't be surprised if you had your own stories where your creativity or your naïve belief that you could do anything was undermined by an event or series of events.

Author and speaker Robert Fulghum has some poignant insight about this loss of creative freedom and unconscious freedom of kids.

Fulghum, author of the best-selling *All I Really Need to Know I Learned in Kindergarten,* was frequently sought out as a speaker, and he often spoke to two groups: kindergartners and college students. He recounted his experience in talking to these beginning and "advanced" learners in his book *Uh-Oh.*

He recalled that when he asked the kindergartners who could sing, all their hands shot up. He would invite them to sing. Don't know the words to the song? "No problem, we make them up." Who can dance? They all could dance. And they danced. He asked how many could draw. They all could draw and proved it with imaginative drawings.

Fulghum writes of this phenomenon: "Their answer is Yes! Over and over again, Yes! The children are confident in spirit, infinite in resources, and eager to learn. Everything is still possible."

When he asked college students the same questions, only a smattering of hands would go up. They said they didn't have the talent. They weren't majoring in those things. They were embarrassed for other people to see them do those things.

At the end of this anecdote, Fulghum asked, "What went wrong between kindergarten and college?"[1]

You can probably point to your own experiences to show what happened. Rules that curtailed creativity. Peer pressure to make you conform to what was "normal" or fashionable at the moment. Naysayers. A misguided teacher scolding you for doing something you thought good or funny or insightful.

I can't help but think of the story that my friend, Melinda Doolittle, told me about the time in fifth grade when she tried out for a choir in St. Louis called Super Gang.

"I wanted to be in that choir so bad," she explained.

The problem was that the choir director, Tom, told Melinda that she couldn't sing. "The note I want and the note you're singing aren't even close," he said. But he loved Melinda's charisma. She energized the choir, so he put her right in the middle but told her not to sing. "Just move your lips."

Melinda was thrilled to be part of the choir, so at first it didn't bother her. But she loved to sing. "In church we're told God gives you the desire of your heart," Melinda said. "And that was my desire."

So after lip-synching in the choir for two years, she decided that she wanted to sing in the talent show put on by her church youth group. Her mom told her to pray long and hard about it, and she told Melinda she would need to practice.

She said singing in the talent show became her faith project. "I wrote it down, and every time I came into my room I saw it."

The night of the show, her singing blew everyone away. "It was a different voice that came out of me. It was truly a gift," she said. From that point on, she said she never looked back. She majored in music at Belmont University and was selected to perform in their prestigious professional showcase with many prominent music labels represented in the audience. She also became a backup singer for big name artists like Aretha Franklin, BeBe and Cece Winans, and Aaron Neville. And you might even remember her placing third in season six of *American Idol*! All this after being told by a choir director that she couldn't sing![2]

We're all so awesomely different. As the psalmist writes, "I am awesomely, wonderfully made." A lot of people don't embrace their differences. In fact, they hide what could make them stand out. Are you one of those people? Would you rather blend in than be known for your unique personality and gifts? Are you wishing that you had different talents? Are you trying to be like others rather than just being yourself? It can be tough to embrace what makes you special, especially if it's not popular. But that's what makes you *you*. So embrace the real you, the *you* that's different from everybody else, and see what happens.

I understand there's a lot of pressure to fit in. As a young kid or grown adult, the pressure to conform is there, to do things that are socially acceptable and culturally popular. To have the things, to wear the things, to go to the places that are "popular" or "cool" or "hip." There's pressure from the media, friends and celebrities, and ourselves.

We dress like our friends, drive similar cars, shop at the same type of stores, eat at the same restaurants. We do these things because we want to fit in and be accepted.

I would argue that those things are okay as long as we're being true to ourselves. It doesn't really matter what type of clothes we wear, unless we're wearing those clothes for the wrong reasons. Are you wearing those clothes just to make you more popular? To help you fit in? To make you feel better about yourself? Are you going to those restaurants because they're the cool places to go, or do you actually like the food there? I've gone to restaurants where I don't even like the food because I believed I was going to see certain people that I wanted to see. I think it's a bit odd that our *desire to be liked* leads us to do things *we don't like*.

Obviously, I'm not immune to that pressure. As a high school and college kid, I knew I didn't want to be drinking, but I would go to these parties where alcohol was the main event. I wanted to at least have a drink in my hand so I would fit in, but really, that was a time when I should have been different. I could have said, "No, I can be at the party without drinking and still have a good time"—and not worried about whether those kids thought I was cool. The times I chose to try to fit in, I always regretted the decisions that came out of it.

There's a time to be unique and let your personality and gifts shine. People who aren't afraid to be different experience great value in the things that they do. They know it takes something extra special to stand apart from the crowd, and they take that risk. They take the chance to be different, even if it means being seen as weird, odd, or abnormal, and they go for it. They are true to who they are. And I guarantee they are rewarded for it. So how can you be true to yourself and still fit in? I say, "Don't fit in. Be different!" Be different when you're called to be different.

More Than a Jock

If your high school was like most, everyone became identified with a certain group: the jocks, the band geeks, the artsy types, the drama crowd, shop kids, the brainiacs, and so on. And rarely did you cross from one group to another.

We tend to give up those things that make us special just to be part of the group. Maybe you are phenomenal at math and it's just not cool to be smart. So you dumb yourself down and pretend like it's hard for you to do, and maybe you even intentionally get some answers wrong on a test—just to fit in. Maybe you're a great singer but none of your friends sing, so you repress that part of yourself and don't join choir because of your friends. But it's your gift! You should use it. And if they are your real friends, they'll support you.

I loved music, but the code said jocks and art don't go together. But I also liked going against the grain, so I played saxophone in our band. From elementary school through high school, I took part in all the school musicals. Not only was it fun to act and sing, I turned out to be pretty good, even landing the lead on two occasions in high school. Though it wasn't the expected thing, being part of the music world allowed me to be even more unique, and it allowed me to diversify my circle of friends. I could have suppressed these talents if I thought they were not as cool as playing football or basketball, but instead I let them show me a new side of life. Stereotypes are made to be broken—there's beauty in being different.

It's in being different that you find out who you truly are and who truly accepts you for who you are. I've seen so many people conform to the way other people say they should be, and they never develop a true sense of self. Being liked because you're like someone else doesn't seem like much of a prize. If people deny their true self, they never experience the joy of being fully themselves. They miss the freedom to laugh at what they think is funny, not what everyone else thinks is funny. There is a unique joy in being successful at what you enjoy doing and what you're good at. There's a freedom in being just who God made you to be and letting those talents show. Maybe that will require you to be different. You may have to step out from what society says is normal or cool. You may have to experience a bit of loneliness to experience who you truly are. But it's well worth it.

You don't have to wear two different shoes and be different on purpose, but I encourage you to not deny the things that make you who you are. Don't conform to the way others say you should be or let cultural pressures hinder your uniqueness. Let those unique characteristics shine. Nurture them. Enhance them. Watch them grow. Watch them bring people into your life who appreciate those things, and they'll say, "I've been looking for someone with your set of skills. I've been looking for someone that's willing to put themselves out there like you have. I've been needing someone who isn't afraid to be different, who isn't afraid to do the things that you can do."

Here's one last story from my high school days about being different, a difference that meant a great deal to me and others.

I was in my senior year and in the college track classes—you know, where you take courses that prepare you for college as opposed to the "vocational" track, often associated with students who the college track kids look down on. Since I was going to college, an English teacher insisted that I take her AP English course. In fact, she insisted I needed her class to get into college. I had other ideas. I took auto shop class. Yeah, I chose to hang out during that time with "grease monkeys" and the shop teacher, Mr. Dix. But I wasn't afraid of being different, and it paid off. I learned so much in Mr. Dix's class. Upon graduation, during my valedictory speech, I gave a shout-out to Mr. Dix. I told the audience, "I got more out of an hour with him than I got out of a whole year of English class."

A couple years ago, I was back at Clarenceville High for my annual football camp, and Mr. Dix, though now retired, happened to be at the school. We bumped into each other in the hallway. Mr. Dix brought up the speech, and I could see he was visibly moved as he talked about it. He said it was one of his proudest moments, to be recognized by a student at commencement. In this case, embracing your difference and talking about it brought an unexpected blessing to one of my favorite teachers.

You will experience those rewarding relationships when you let yourself be you. You will learn to appreciate the way

God has made you, and that He's given you unique gifts to use to allow you to stand out and make a difference in the lives of others.

So embrace your uniqueness; you will shine.

Display your talents; you will be fulfilled.

Pour out your passion; the world will become a better place when you do.

Self-confidence vs. Self-consciousness

Now this is going to sound odd, even puzzling: in spite of always being self-confident, I was, growing up, also self-conscious. Like many kids, I felt especially self-conscious through my teenage years. I believed that I was being viewed and judged constantly, and although sports was an area of great confidence for me, it also magnified the opinions of others about me. What I thought about myself became less important than what others thought, and this caused me to have some real struggles. Managing other people's opinions is something we all deal with, and it's an area I have had to learn to deal with my whole life.

Often we think that confidence and insecurity are flip-sides of the same coin, but I believe you can have strong self-confidence while also struggling with issues of self-consciousness. I've been told that I operate with an assuredness of who I am and what I'm capable of, but that doesn't mean I've never worried about what other people think of me. It didn't take long to figure out that other people were watching me.

Once, in middle school, I was sent to the office with a written description of my offense—my teacher clearly didn't appreciate my sense of humor. I was sure she was wrong. The vice principal, a short little man with a short mustache and a short temper, wasn't pleased with my unrepentant attitude. He stormed out of the office mumbling, "By God..." He returned a moment later and handed me warm, freshly photocopied sheets of paper. On them were two definitions from Webster's dictionary, one from the *s*'s and one from the *c*'s. One word was highlighted on each page. Words that stuck with me for quite some time. *Smug* and *conceited*. I didn't believe that I was those things the vice principal labeled me, but I knew that if he thought that about me, others probably did as well. I didn't like it.

From where I stood, I was just being me. It's not that I was cocky, I was just trying to figure out how to be me. I carried myself in a way that made people think that I was smug or conceited. It took my middle school vice principal to open my eyes to the way other people saw me. What really bothered me was that it was my own actions that were causing people to see me that way. I tried to pretend that I didn't care, but what other people thought of me mattered.

Even as my athletic success continued, early in high school I still struggled with others' opinions. As the attention increased, I realized that I couldn't control what everyone thought—I could only control my words and actions.

I could make a conscious effort to be nice and treat people well, but at the end of the day, they were going to think what they were going to think. It didn't matter how many times I was in the paper, or that I scored 135 touchdowns. I learned to be myself and left others to their own opinions. True, I still put some self-worth in my performance and what others thought, but like quitting a bad habit, I was worrying about what other people thought of me less and less.

My final step to freedom from concern over others' opinions was the realization that only God can judge me. As a pro, I stopped worrying about what people thought of my performance. I knew I couldn't please them all—fans, coaches, or the media. People will praise you one day and curse you the next. Until that realization, I had been more concerned with my image. I wanted to be seen as a hard working good guy. I wanted to be known as a leader and someone of importance. I believe it all came down to my need for love and acceptance.

I was worried that I looked like a conceited athlete. I thought that having a certain car would give me the wrong appearance. I was concerned about being seen at the wrong place by the wrong people and what that might do to my image. My mindset was all wrong. I needed to be guided by my own conscience. I needed to stop letting anything else dictate my actions and start trusting myself to do what was best. I started to trust myself and my motives instead of worrying about what those actions would look like. Once I was able to redirect my mindset this way, I was free from the opinions and expectations. Maybe more importantly, I became free from what I assumed others were thinking. That freedom allowed me to be my true self and make decisions in alignment with my desires and values.

Once you have achieved this status, where your approval is the only one that matters, you now have what I call the "I don't give a pile of manure (or some other related term) what you think" attitude. Now, hold on, I know what you're thinking. That attitude doesn't sound very high character or even nice. Well, I don't mean it in the stuck-up, mean way it may sound. I mean it in a self-confident, empowering way. This attitude is a way of saying, "I know myself, and I'm confident that I'll do what is right." There will always be voices from the outside. Some will be positive and helpful, but some will be negative and harmful. When you've embraced the true you, you don't let the positives get you up or the negatives get you down. You can't control the outside voices, so listen to your own true voice. Even the voices of loved ones that you have learned to trust shouldn't undermine the true voice inside you. This doesn't mean that you're never wrong or that you can't take criticism. It means that after all the voices have been heard, you know that the path you choose will be the one for you. And if you're wrong, you will correct it in due time and learn from it.

Two Shoe Remix

While I was in the NFL, I had a Nike shoe contract, so I had access to a bunch of shoes that I could mix and match. I came to the obvious conclusion that I should bring back my first-grade fashion statement! It would be a return to that time of unconstrained creativity. Who knows? I may even start a trend. This whole idea sprang up after I read Malcolm Gladwell's *The Tipping Point*. In the book, he related how a popular group of kids from Manhattan single-handedly resurrected Hushpuppies, a shoe that had gone from being "the every man's shoe" to being "the old man's shoe." The brand was dead, then all of a sudden this group of kids brought the brand back to the forefront of style. While some people are connectors and others are mavens, or experts, these kids were influencers, according to Gladwell.[3] I wanted to know if I too was an influencer. So my social experiment (a joke really) began.

I remember the first day as an adult I went out in public wearing two different colored shoes—same style, but one was mostly red, the other mostly blue. I assure you, still stylish. I walked into the bank in downtown Highland Park, a suburb of Chicago, and I remember the looks from the bank's two employees.

"Do you know you have two different shoes on?" the assistant manager asked.

"Yeah," I said. "It's awesome, isn't it? You should try it."

He was wearing a nice pair of brown dress shoes with his bank attire. I continued, "You could wear two different dress shoes. It would be awesome."

The teller didn't share my enthusiasm.

Every time I wear two different shoes, I get looks of puzzlement, amusement, sometimes approval, and sometimes hostility.

One day, I was at a wedding and an older woman kept glancing at my two different shoes. Finally, unable to help herself, she approached me and said, "Why do you do that?"

"Why not?" I said, grinning. "Don't you like it?"

"No," she replied curtly and walked away.

Clearly, if you're a bit different, not everyone is going to appreciate it—or your sense of humor.

I may not have started a two-different shoes trend—but I have noticed a two-different socks trend. Coincidence? Or trend setting? Ha! In any case, I sure have had a lot of fun being different, and I have a lot of stories to tell because of it. In fact, nowadays, people ask me why I *don't* have two different shoes on. Now we are getting somewhere!

Whiteboard Goals: Be Different

Your assignment for this chapter, "should you choose to accept it," is to be different. Be different because it says something about who you are. Are all your friends getting tattoos? Be different and don't. Everybody binge watching the latest, hottest show? Sign up for that photography class or writing workshop or online business class instead. Coworkers on a perpetual "casual Friday" dress code every day? Dress up. Dress for success. Write down how you will be different in the coming weeks (or months). Be different, and let that difference push you toward your goals.

BLITZ YOUR
PASSION

4
TALENT MEETS HEART

Wherever you needed him, on the field or off, Spider was there. Broken chin strap in the middle of a game? You would see him hustling down the sideline with his long strides, a forward lean to his body—the result of childhood scoliosis— giving the impression he was on a mission that couldn't wait. As he reached you, his hands would already be in his tool belt. A turn of a screwdriver here, a snap there, a slap on the helmet, and you were back in the game before the next snap of the ball. Ripped pants? An extra pair or, in an emergency, a safety pin. A size 17 shoe blowout? No problem. A replacement was coming right up.

As Penn State's equipment manager, Brad "Spider" Caldwell was responsible for the equipment needs of more than 100 football players, including 2,000 jerseys, 2,000 cleats, and on-the-spot replacement, adjustment, or repair of malfunctioning gear during a game. It wasn't unusual for Brad to work eighty-hour weeks during football season. All who saw him could tell his talents—mechanical and organizational—were aligned with his heart and a passion for service.

When Brad was in junior high, the eighth-grade football coach thought Brad had the right personality and asked him to be manager. He agreed, though reluctantly. Soon, he was manager for the high school team. And in 1983, Brad enrolled at Penn State and became the football team's student manager. From there, he became assistant equipment manager and then head equipment manager, a role he held for more than thirty years until his retirement.[1]

Looking back at my days as a member of the Penn State football team, I see that Brad poured his heart into his work; he had a passion for what he did. "But wait," you say. "We're talking equipment manager—he got you water, made sure your uniform was clean, fixed equipment. What's the big deal? It's not like he was a CEO."

Here's the big deal: He was a success. Brad found something that brought him fulfillment. Success isn't defined by a job title—I'm sure there are scores of CEOs and company presidents that don't feel fulfilled. In fact, they may be downright miserable. They have pursued money but not their passion.

So how important was Brad Caldwell to the Penn State football program? Several years ago, a couple of writers, Lou Prato and Scott Brown, wrote a book called *What It Means to Be a Nittany Lion,* which profiled the top 68 Penn

State football players going back to the 1930s. Brad had been the equipment manager for thirty of those players, and he had known twenty others. He passed on his knowledge about the players to the writers, thinking he was providing them background information. When the book came out, Brad looked at the last chapter, which included three non-player "Honorable Mentions." To his surprise, following the profiles of some of the greatest Penn State players over eight decades, he saw his own profile. Brown, the book's coauthor, said that including Brad was an easy call because he was such a big part of Penn State football history. Reflecting on his time from when he first became a manager at Penn State, Brad said, "I never dreamed that twenty-five years later I would have the keys to Beaver Stadium."[2] In 2015, Brad came out of retirement to become the facilities coordinator at Beaver Stadium. But he still has his tool pouch nearby. "I'm keeping it close, just in case."[3]

That's the kind of thing that happens when your skills and talents align with your passion. Passion impacts. It has to. When we pursue things with passion, people notice and are changed. It's obvious when people are pursuing their passion. They can't hide and they don't want to. It's actually not what they are doing that is so impactful and contagious, but it's the way they are doing it. They might do it so well or so energetically, or so gracefully or effortlessly that others can't help but be inspired.

For Brad, it's as if the role of equipment manager chose him. "I was meant to do this," he said. I know that feeling.

Often I have said it's as if football chose me instead of the other way around. I didn't decide that football was my passion, it just was. I know how lucky I was to have found my passion at twelve years old. It was a natural relationship, me and football. The only question was how long our relationship would last.

I loved it from the first day I put shoulder pads on as a sixth grader. Sure, there were times it was tough to pursue, literal aches and pains, mental and emotional strains, and many sacrifices along the way. But I never wanted to quit. Football pumped me up. It brought joy; it brought energy and life. This outweighed any discomfort or inconvenience. I had to make choice after choice to excel and push myself, but it was always what I wanted, so it didn't seem like much of a reach. By no means was it easy, but by all means it was natural.

Pursuing football was to be on fire. Pursuing the game ignited all I was doing. I lit up when I thought about it or talked about it. My passion was contagious. It spilled into my work ethic. It showed in my school spirit and impacted people around the school, and it exploded on the field and impacted my teammates.

I've seen examples of this kind of passion in other people throughout my life. As you know by now, I love golf. And once in a while, I'll come across a greenskeeper who loves his job, a job he's gifted to do. That greenskeeper who is fulfilled with his or her job knows it's not just about cutting the grass short. It's about the right amount of fertilizer, the right amount of water, the mixture of soils, when to aerate, when to overseed, and many other details of which I'm not even aware. Their skills and talents have obviously met their passion.

Creative Ringmaster

Both my parents provided excellent examples of people using their skills and talents in pursuit of their passion; both found lives of fulfillment.

I see my father's gifts and abilities in the way he taught kids. It is obvious that his talent has met his heart when he is telling stories about his years as an educator, when he is pouring his passion into someone else.

To say my dad was simply an elementary school librarian would be understating his role. In my mind, he was more like a Ringmaster of Creativity. His tools for learning included any number of activities, such as puppet shows, a student-produced daily television show, and history simulations.

His creative activities proved to be most impactful for students most in need of help. His puppets helped two special students; we'll call them Tough Teddy and Quiet Courtney.

Tough Teddy's speech was very difficult to understand. When Teddy visited the library, he and the other students were encouraged to pick up one of the puppets Dad had scattered throughout the room. Dad encouraged Teddy to create conversations with his puppet, a dog he named Scruffy. He also made an exception to allow Tough Teddy to take Scruffy home. Because Teddy became more verbal during his interactions with the dog puppet, his parents bought him a real dog they named Scruffy. "The puppet," Dad said, "freed up his voice so we could understand him."

Quiet Courtney was a selective mute. In other words, she would talk at home, but since the time she had entered kindergarten, Courtney had chosen not to talk at school. The school counselor asked Dad to help with a puppet activity. Dad had a puppet theater in the library. Kids would duck down behind a curtain and have their puppets enact a story. Not only did the puppet allow Quiet Courtney to talk, but she was able to adapt a number of different puppet voices for the theatre. For their big puppet show, other adults and kids from the school were invited. At the end of the show, when the kids came out from behind the screen for their curtain call, there stood a smiling Courtney. "You should have seen the surprise on everybody's face when they saw her," Dad said. "'That was Quiet Courtney!'" As Courtney progressed through school, she did eventually find her voice. I'm sure Dad, in his own small way, contributed to that.

Dad also had his elementary students do a daily television show with anchors, reporters, and camera operators. For example, one year the role of reporter went to a very special student we will call Joyful James. Every week he would present the facts about one of the states. Even when the semester ended, because James was autistic and depended on routine, Dad allowed him to continue with his state reporting. However, when the school year was coming to an end, the teachers were concerned about Joyful James moving up to middle school. Would he be able to cope with this big change? Dad and his colleagues had an idea: send Joyful James ahead of the other students as an investigative reporter for the television show. That's exactly what they did. James came back and reported on all that he had seen.

"I'll never forget his report," Dad said. "He ended with, 'I have to tell you, I *didn't* like middle school. (Pause) I LOVED IT!'"

What Dad will be remembered for most, he said, are the simulations. He would decorate and use costumes and props in the library to reenact important events. He took students to the moon, participated in the Iditarod dog race, journeyed through time, and visited Alice in Wonderland, with Dad playing the Mad Hatter.

"The one kids remember most," he said, "was the Underground Railroad." Dad dressed as Peg Leg Joe and had the kids hide in the dark in cupboards or between bookcases with an improvised roof. Someone on the outside with a stick would bang on bookcases and call out, "Anybody in there?"

"To see their faces—the kids would be terrified," he said. It really helped them understand just how scary that time was.

Listening to my dad tell these stories, I could tell how much he loved what he did. He had the skills, the creativity, and the passion for his work.

A Baby-Shaped Hole

My mother is another great example. She describes herself as having a baby-shaped hole in her heart—she loves nurturing and caring for babies. I guess the four boys she gave birth to weren't enough, because around the time I was in first grade, Mom started taking care of foster babies. In nurturing the babies from birth to adoption, usually just a month or two, Momma Shaw let her talents shine. She had a magical way with babies. She often got them to sleep through the night earlier than most babies do. And she poured her life into them. All fifty-something of them. That's right, over twenty-one years, we had more than fifty babies stay with us for a time.

Growing up, it was normal for us to have a baby in tow. Every concert or game, the baby came along. We all helped out, but it was Momma Shaw whose passion was on display. (An added bonus: when I was at school with the baby, all the girls came to see.)

My mother never received accolades for all she did for those babies. She was never compensated for what she did. In fact, it cost her money, time, and tears. But that's not why she did it. She did it because it was her gift. She followed her gift with passion. And all who saw her with a baby could tell. She could have ignored that gift and pushed it aside for something that paid, but that wouldn't have been her true self, and the world would have been denied her passion.

Sadly, it seems that most people don't pursue their passion. Many sacrifice their dream for a job that provides a more stable lifestyle. They would rather have security than have their heart filled. This sacrifice may be for a noble purpose, but at the end of the day, your noble cause may become an excuse to keep you from moving forward. It is not wrong to sacrifice, but dreams are made to be fulfilled.

You must find purpose in your sacrifice and ultimately find a way to negotiate between taking care of your responsibilities and stepping out to pursue your dream. It doesn't have to be a choice of one or the other. You can do both, but it requires a bit of risk, and it will take your full attention as you turn your mind to pursuing a life of passion and purpose.

Have you personally witnessed someone pursuing his or her passion? Are you living your life out that way? Or are you chasing something other than your passion, using something other than your talents and abilities? If so, you are missing out. And also the world is missing out. What the world needs is for you to do what you do best. For you to use and share your gifts, to align those talents with your heart. Figure out what you desire and what you are good at. And that's when our lives start to take off and great things start to happen.

This is what football was for me for a long time. God gave me gifts and abilities athletically—to run, to hit, to compete, to lead. And when those things were being used, you could see my heart and my passion in them. I cared so much about what I was doing. I poured everything into it. And those emotions and desires aligned with my gifts and abilities. That's what created success. It was a big contributor to the impact I was able to have through the world of sports.

We are all searching for a purpose. Oftentimes people are going through life searching for something that matters, something that means something. I believe that purpose may not be as hard to find as you think. It may be as simple as a redirection of your talents, a shift in focus, or honing in on your passion.

Star Trainer

Stacey Daniels is one such person. I first met Stacey when another Titans player and I helped him with a football combine he was running for high school kids. After that brief encounter, we saw each other again later in the week at a church service. We hit it off and became fast friends. Since then, we've joined forces to start a company that teaches performance and wellness, character and leadership. But how Stacey got to Nashville and started his own fitness training company called SD Performance is a great story.

Stacey wanted to be a professional soccer player. Growing up, he spent all his time and effort pursuing that goal. However, at the end of his college career, he was burned out. But he had a lifetime of athletic experience, and he put his skills and abilities to work by becoming a graduate assistant performance specialist for IMG Academy in Bradenton, Florida.

It was a job he loved. "I busted my butt working with athletes and kids," he said.

At the end of his assistantship, two full-time trainers had left, but when he went to apply, he was told there wasn't room to hire another person.

He ended up going home to Connecticut, but he didn't give up. He regularly e-mailed people at IMG Academy, including the performance director, saying that he was still interested in a job. Eight months later, they offered him a part-time position.

Even though it was part time, he spent as much time there as if he were full time. "I hung out at the performance center every available moment," Stacey said. "Any person. Any sport. If someone needed help, I'd jump in to help train."

His passion didn't go unrecognized. The performance director called him in and said, "I just want to let you know you've gone above and beyond." Stacey was hired full time and later became assistant director of the department. During his time at IMG, he trained NFL running back Chris Johnson for the 2008 combine, where Johnson ran the 40-yard dash in 4.24 seconds, setting the record for his position. Stacey also trained such elite athletes as Zac Stacy, Tony Romo, Byron Leftwich, Dominique Rodgers-Cromartie, and Luke Kuechly, all of the NFL. From the NBA, he trained Vince Carter, Chauncey Billups, and Tayshaun Prince. Major League Baseball's Dex Fowler of the 2016 World Series Champions, Joey Votto, and Ian Desmond were on his list, as well as pro tennis players Tommy Haas, Kei Nishikori, and Jelena Janković. In addition, Stacey trained the Under-17 National Soccer Team, developing future stars such as Eddie Johnson, Freddy Adu, Jozy Altidore, Kellyn Acosta, Omar Gonzalez, and Michael Bradley.

Stacey's passion and success opened the door for him to eventually start his own training center in Nashville.

Sometimes a more massive shift in focus may be necessary, like that of Morris Chapman, who I told you about earlier. Morris, as you recall, went from janitor to recording artist and worship leader. Like Morris, you need to let your talents, abilities, and heart guide you toward something that will be more fulfilling and engage your true gifts. Talents, abilities, and gifts are great indicators of where you may find purpose. That purpose, as you may have noted from the examples I've presented, always extends beyond oneself.

Your abilities have the power to better the world around you, enhance your life, and help others along the way. In fact, I argue that you can't help but better the world as you go. It's a natural side effect of pursuing your best.

People don't pursue their passion simply for an external prize, but because life itself lies within it and fulfillment is its consequence. Maybe even more so, without the pursuit of that thing there is a void. Yet, even with this gaping hole, many people manage to carry on, pretending or ignoring it. The size of the hole doesn't compare to the fear of failure and being uncomfortable. So they accept life without their passion and live with the fear and the void. The choice to settle not only keeps them from a full life but deprives others from experiencing their gift.

This is the world we live in: the majority of people are not pursuing their passion. It's as if we believe that only a select lucky few get permission to do so. And we aren't the ones. We're the ones whose situation doesn't allow for dream chasing. We have too much responsibility. We would if we could, but circumstances don't allow. Or so it seems. But what if we didn't see it that way? What if the majority of us, regardless of circumstances, actually pursued our passion?

The world would thrive. More people would be doing what they love and loving what they do. And the outcome would be staggering. Productivity and quality would skyrocket. Because, yes, you are a pretty good salesperson, but you were called to be a cabinet maker or sculptor or math teacher and a mentor to kids. Your life would shine and impact people, but you can't step away from the six-figure comfort. So you settle for being a pretty good salesperson. But when you leave what is comfortable and average for what is uncomfortable and amazing, you excel and life expands. The pursuit of your passion changes so much. You are no longer going to work, you are pursuing something you care about. Your attitude changes for the better. A better attitude and a life on fire is contagious. So now you have bettered yourself and inspired another to do the same. You are producing a better product, whatever that is, because you care more. Your attitude is better and life in general is better.

You find that as you pursue your passion you connect with others who are pursuing their passion. You inspire each other. You find your wanting of trivial things decreases as the desire for things that fuel or complement your pursuit increases. People and things that detract from your purpose are less and less attractive; you realize they are time wasters. You find your true priorities, and they are not the burden they once were.

Life seems to be flowing not only toward, but out of your passion. Your thoughts and energy draw toward it and you get new ideas from it. And others are doing the same. It's as if you are on your path and they are on theirs. Though the paths can overlap, it's only to enhance each other through competition or encouragement. There is competition but not conflict. You know that your path is for you.

Life isn't perfect just because you and a lot of others have committed to chasing your passion. There are still trials, pain, and heartbreak. These are to grow you and make you better. But these tough things are now worth it. They aren't meaningless or simply to make ends meet, but they are to get to something that matters, something that you care about. There are still people doing wrong and disrupting the good in the world. We can only strive and hope to influence them positively, that they would discover their passion as well.

Don't discredit your dream. It may seem illogical to others, but if your desire is strong enough, then you should strive to make it happen. Passion is a scary thing. It comes with all types of emotions. Passion changes and challenges people. It can lead to ridicule and embarrassment. It sounds dangerous or even dumb. So why would anyone pursue passion?

Because it brings life and hope.

Whiteboard Goals: Get a Plan

You've identified your passion, your crazy dream. You've written that down and you've started that journey. Now, ask yourself what additional skills and abilities you may need to accomplish those goals. *How* are you going to attain those skills and abilities? Will that require extra hours of practice, formal or informal courses, relocation, a second job, extra reading? Whatever that is, formulate a plan and write it down. Keep it handy to make sure you're making progress toward your goals. And one more assignment: If at all possible, write an e-mail to someone who is doing what you want to do. Ask for advice or a meeting where you could discuss your mutual passion. Networking, finding like-minded people, is a fine tool to help you achieve your dreams.

5

A PLAYBOOK OF PASSIONATE PURSUITS

Over the past chapters, I've written about looking within ourselves and finding out who we are and what we value. I've talked about embracing our differences and standing out. Through my experiences and the experiences of others, I've shown what a life of passion can look like. Now, let's examine what all those facets can look like in the following individuals. These are people I know personally. One reason I picked them is to show that you don't have to go far to find stories of success and inspiration. They're in your circles of friends too. My point is, these are regular people. They didn't start out with a lot of money. They weren't deemed geniuses—in fact, one of my friends even had a learning disability. But they had a passion, a vision, and a desire to impact the world.

So I'm calling these "A Playbook of Passionate Pursuits." I think you'll find plenty to study and admire, even emulate.

From the Ground Up

How does a home-schooled, twenty-year-old woman go from living in her car to becoming CEO of the largest social venture real estate company in Nashville, with $50 million in revenue and $95 million dollars in projects?

The short answer: passion. The longer answer, the particulars of her story, are fascinating and instructive, reflecting many of the points I've been making.

I first met Britnie when we were speaking to a group of students at an event called Summit at Lipscomb University in Nashville. We became friends, and over the last couple years, I've learned more about her story. It's an impressive one, I'm sure you'll agree.

Britnie grew up in North Augusta, South Carolina, and at the age of twelve decided she wanted to be a missionary to Africa. In high school Britnie worked five jobs to pay for her travel costs for an Africa mission trip.

"I knew I was going to be poor," she says. "I was going to live in a mud hut doing missions. Being poor is just how it works."

Britnie had a deep desire to help but knew she needed the skills to make a real impact, so she enrolled in a leadership school called Morningstar University.

"It's 50 percent ministry training, 50 percent survival school," Britnie explained. "Our team, called Special Forces, had Green Berets and survivalists train us for a year." Their first survivalist trip was a surprise seventy-mile hike on the Appalachian Trail with no gear or food. "I lost almost twenty-five pounds in four days," she said.

At the age of seventeen, Britnie and her Special Forces team went on a mission trip to Costa Rica. During the women's conference her team put on, Britnie met a young girl who had been sexually abused by her father. It was socially acceptable in this region for fathers to "break in their daughters." The girl was now handicapped and so traumatized she had no ability to speak.

"I've never seen such hopelessness in someone's eyes. It's a look I will never forget. I realized she didn't even have a chance to do anything like I was doing—what you can do in your sleep in America," she says. "I decided then I wanted to close the gap and create opportunity for those who had none. And I will fight until this atrocity is no longer socially acceptable."

One day back in the States, the school brought a speaker to class. He asked how many had gone on mission trips. Britnie raised her hand. Then he asked how many had to raise funds in order to go. She raised her hand again. And then he said, "Do you know you can buy a house with no money down? If your mortgage payment is $900 a month, and you rent it for $1,200, you get to keep that $300. Do that ten times, and you won't ever have to send out those begging letters to fund your missions."

So at eighteen, she bought her first house. In the process of buying it she heard you could flip houses and make chunks of money. If you save those chunks of money, you could build an entire orphanage and not have to ask anyone else for money. She decided then she would never stop until she could be financially independent to be able to fund her calling. So she set out to learn everything about real estate and flipping houses, but she said nothing was working. It was 2008, and everything she touched seemed to fail. She ended up having to wait tables, working every double shift she could just to make her mortgage payment. One night, a couple came in and sat in her section of the restaurant. Britnie noticed that the man was wearing a ring with a house logo on the side with the words "The Millionaire's Club."

The couple, as it turned out, put on real estate training conferences. Britnie said she was going to be a real estate investor, which they didn't take seriously. What did a twenty-year-old know about real estate? But as they talked they found out how much reading and research she had been doing, so they invited her to their next conference. At that conference she used the last available dollars on her credit cards to take the speakers out to dinner so she could pick their brains about the business. She overheard one of them telling another speaker that he needed an assistant who could learn the business and manage his projects as he ran his speaking career. Pumped about the opportunity to learn, she accepted a position even though she would be making less than the minimums on her credit card bills at the time. Two weeks later she moved to Nashville; thirty days later they eliminated the position altogether. She had been surviving on her credit cards and had a debt of $35,000.

A PLAYBOOK OF PASSIONATE PURSUITS

"That day I got fired is the day I met these two guys who rehabbed houses," Britnie said. She asked them if she could work for them for free in exchange for learning the business. They agreed and she hit the ground running, working eighteen-plus hours a day. She had to live in her car on and off for nine months. "Survival school was a huge help," she said.

During the time she worked for free, Britnie said she got her real estate license and learned how to find deals and manage crews. She worked on multiple projects and made the people teaching her a ton of money, she said. Finally, in 2011, at the age of twenty-two, she did her first home rehab by herself. When the deal closed, it made $40,000. Then she did two rehabs, then four. In the first year and a half of business, she did more than one hundred projects!

This is, of course, an amazing success story. It's a story of perseverance and overcoming obstacles. But remember, her passion was for African missions and making an impact. She was going to quit real estate at age twenty-six, but she realized that it was a tool that could be used to change the world. She didn't abandon her passion but used her skills to fund and make her passion possible. I respect this a ton; she didn't jump ship for the money. As she grew her business, Britnie made several trips to Africa and partnered with an organization called Horizon Initiative, which was making an impact in Kenya through its mission of rescuing and empowering orphaned children through a self-sustaining micro-community model.

Britnie, now a board member of Horizon Initiative, said she saw that when they built an orphanage, it transformed the whole area. Here's how it works: a six- to twelve-acre site is anchored by a children's home (an orphanage), farming plots, on-site trade schools, and other small-business ventures. For example, a sewing center makes their own uniforms and sells additional clothing to the community, the poultry farm provides eggs for the kids, and the extra eggs are sold at the market.

She decided that transforming Nashville's urban core would be practice for her long-term vision of helping to create economic stability in developing nations.

The way to change a neighborhood, she said, is to first get the criminal activity out so the area has a chance to change. Her company works closely with the police department, requesting special attention be paid to targeted areas. Next, they clean up the area, literally.

"We'll get out there with trash bags and clean up the place," she said. "We aren't going to own the whole street—we don't want to, but once it's clean people start taking pride in their neighborhood." Additionally, they'll help the elderly renovate their homes or build ramps for them so they can safely access their homes.

They clean up the "grunge" from the neighborhood—homes that aren't historic—and do so in a concentrated manner. In a three-square-block area, for example, they built seventy-nine new homes. The change in the neighborhood attracts more investments, businesses, restaurants, and jobs all resulting in opportunity for people.

Not only are they transforming neighborhoods, Britnie said, they're addressing social needs through their developments. A big project on the board, North Lights, is a twenty-three-acre development that includes a mix of affordable cottages, single-family homes, apartments, and retail space with the goal of integrating arts into real estate and creating a sanctuary for art and innovation. This project will enable artists to be able to continue living in Nashville, which makes Nashville a better place all around. They also have a project named East Greenway Park that has a greenway connection. "It's the first totally dedicated health and wellness community in Nashville." Britnie said to bless the neighborhood, they're donating $100,000 to build sidewalks—not even on their property—to give neighbors access to the fifteen-mile-long greenway and the 960-acre park called Shelby Bottoms.

But all this success almost didn't happen. If living in your car isn't enough of an obstacle, how about an associate stealing one million dollars just as the business is taking off?

A contractor she had worked with kept going over budget on the home renovations she was working on. "Everything blew up the day I told him he can't keep going over budget," Britnie said. "He was the one to create the budgets in the first place." In addition to overcharging for each project, it turned out that he hadn't paid his subcontractors in three months. On top of that, he was using a computer program to make fake building permits.

"I had to rip out electrical systems, tear off entire additions," Britnie said. She didn't know how her investors would ever trust her again with this happening on her watch. "I wanted to curl up and die I was so stressed. I didn't know which subcontractors he had paid and who had not been paid. So there was a lot of crying happening throughout the day," she said. "But every time I wanted to quit, I closed my eyes and I could see that little girl's face in Costa Rica—I literally saw her eyes."

Britnie said she constantly told herself, "This has never been about you or money, this is about creating a way for others! Go shove some makeup back on to hide those tears, get back out there, and figure this out!"

Britnie put her boots on and went to the jobsites everyday until she figured it all out. She managed to get everyone paid and get the jobs done right. Instead of her investors bailing out on her, she said they actually invested more with her. "They realized I had their backs no matter what."

Her passion for missions has taken her on a fulfilling journey. Not only has it brought her recognition—named one of 2014's Entrepreneurial Winning Women by Ernst and Young, *Glamour* magazine's Hometown Hero and 2015 Enterprising Woman of the Year, *Forbes* magazine's number six in the world for fastest growing woman-owned company, *Fortune* magazine's number three in the nation for fastest growing inner city company, Best in Business, Woman of Influence, Top 10 most powerful women in Nashville, and an invited speaker to the United Nations' Global Diversity Leadership Exchange—but it has brought socially responsible change to Nashville and a proven model for change in developing countries.

"Give me a rough area, and we'll work to make it awesome. We'll figure it out."

Trombone Magic

Of course, a passionate pursuit doesn't have to involve professional sports, fame, or business success. You can make an impact in the lives of others through significant, though less visible, ways.

As an example, I think of my older brother Steve. He is the oldest of four boys, and while all four of us were always into sports, we also played instruments through our school years, but Steve made music his passion. Like most kids, he started band in elementary school—in fifth grade he started playing trombone. And if you've ever played an instrument, you know how much work it takes to get better. Weekly lessons. Daily practicing. Playing scales over and over. And then there's that first band performance. And all the different instruments come together. Songs start sounding like songs. You realize that music is satisfying. Powerful even. And then you're hooked.

So it went with Steve until, in high school, he became drum major, went to drum major camp, and pushed his passion to a new level. As drum major, you were the "conductor" on the field, responsible for keeping cadence, initiating songs and formations on the field, and selecting and directing the pep band in the bleachers.

"As a senior in high school," Steve said, "I was in band twice a day, choir twice a day, and I went to the middle school to work with their band kids."

In college, Steve auditioned for drum major, a highly coveted position in the Central Michigan University marching band. "While all the other candidates were silently vocalizing the counts, I yelled out the counts," Steve said. That confidence, that passion, made him stand out—and win the drum major gig.

I remember visiting Steve when he was in college—even though he was just a year and a half older, he was three grades ahead of me, having started school a year early and also skipping a grade. As I tagged along across campus, in the dorm halls, the cafeteria, and the classroom building, I saw how students greeted Steve, with friendship, respect, and enthusiasm. If I had ever thought of Steve as a "band geek," I now realized he was Mr. College. BMOC. Man, I was so proud of him.

Success, of course, leads to more success. And Steve, as a music major, just kept getting better and better. He decided he wanted to pursue a master's degree while making music his career as a band instructor.

"I did entertain the idea of going into ministry, but I also realized that I can impact lives as a teacher, especially when I can see kids for seven or eight years in a row, from the time they start lessons through high school," Steve said.

Over the years, Steve has added just about every musical instrument to his repertoire: French horn and trumpet, guitar, flute, clarinet, sax, oboe—anything an elementary or middle school kid could want to play. As the band director in Freeland, Michigan, Steve shares his passion with elementary, middle school, and high school students.

Steve said that as the band director, it's "teaching life through music." Being part of a band takes teamwork, collaboration, and respect for each other's abilities, Steve points out. Students have to be responsible and show up on time, practice time management, and practice on their own. In my mind, that sounds a lot like being part of a sports team. (And music is something you can do for a lifetime, not just until you're thirtysomething.)

In addition to all those life skills, Steve said it still comes down to the power of music. "Sometimes the only way for students—or anybody for that matter—to express themselves is through music. Music brings smiles to people's faces. Music can create drama and tension. There's an emotional and spiritual response to music. For me, it's a big part of my faith; it draws me closer to God."

That's the kind of passion Steve brings to his students. And yes, he said, he sometimes has to combat the "it's only band" comment. "I tell my students they have to decide what they love to do. They can't let negative comments affect them. You have to find what that passion is for you."

I guess this passion thing runs in the family.

Tech Jam

Another friend, entrepreneur, and leader in the servant-leader mold is Marcus Cobb. Not surprisingly, being in Nashville, Marcus's company is involved in the music industry, and he is also an amateur musician. In fact, we connected because of music. We shared a stage at a mutual friend's house. We collaborated on our unique version of "Ain't No Sunshine." He sang and I displayed my lyrical rapping genius.

Marcus started Jammber, a company that streamlines paperwork and gets everyone involved in a music project paid more quickly. For example, because of the inefficiency and complexity of the music industry's outdated paper-tracking systems, it can take nearly two years for a guitarist to get paid for a single recording session worth a few hundred dollars. They speed things up by having their clients schedule creative projects through their website, and Jammber automatically generates all the required paperwork electronically, including union forms and tax forms, allowing electronic signatures and quick payments.

When you hear his story, how he survived a horrendous childhood, overcame obstacles, and achieved goals to become the leader of successful companies, touching the lives of thousands, you'll understand why he says of his past, "I hate to say that it was worth it, but I'll say it's for the better."

I think you'll find his path to success inspiring and his comments on leadership encouraging.

Marcus was born in El Paso, Texas. His mom was seventeen and unmarried; his father was older but had been an alcoholic since the age of twelve. In the late seventies, he says El Paso was one of the most dangerous cities at that time. "It was all about gangs and gang affiliation, almost as bad as LA. There were streets you could not cross, and there were constant shootings."

Marcus tells about the time when he was eight or nine years old and walked out onto the porch in his pajamas and saw his Uncle Charles's beautiful Fleetwood Cadillac. "I saw bullet holes all up and down the car. They were celebrating because they had a shootout with the cops the night before."

His uncle lost an eye in the shootout, and he was lifting the patch to show everyone. They were drinking and toasting his eye. "That's how hard core they were. That's the environment I grew up in."

In spite of that atmosphere, Marcus was a good student, interested in books. He said he rarely left the library, or he would bargain with the Bookmobile librarian to check out more books than typically allowed. Also, because his cousins and uncles were OGs—Original Gangsters—they were able to protect him from being recruited by gangs. He didn't know it at the time, but he was hands-off.

Even so, he had other problems. His stepfather, a crack addict, would get high and beat the crap out of him from the time he was seven until he was sixteen. "I was physically abused by my stepfather, and then for stints I was sexually abused by one of our neighbors, an older boy, who was in turn being sexually abused by his uncle."

When he was thirteen, he ran away with another friend and hid in the massive sewers and reservoirs of El Paso. Friends would sneak them food. He says he was so happy because he couldn't get beaten. "But I did get tired. On day seven, we walked back to my middle school. Of course, everyone was looking for these kids. They called my parents and Social Services."

As in the past, whenever Social Services got involved, they would move. Over the years, Marcus went to a couple different elementary schools, three middle schools, and six different high schools. But he was still a straight-A student and played basketball. He built his first robot when he was seven years old. When he was eleven, he tried to order neon gas to build a laser. The man he was talking to asked, "Sir, how old are you?" Marcus told him he was eleven. "Do you know neon gas can kill you? Can I talk to your parents?" He didn't build a laser, but he wrote his first computer game when he was twelve or thirteen.

After the family moved to get away from Social Services, the beatings started again about six months later. One day after school, his cousin Creighton took his backpack and took out Marcus's journal. He was going to tease him because he thought Marcus was writing about some girl he liked. Actually, it was a journal of his nearly daily beatings, which his stepfather made him keep. Creighton started flipping through the pages.

"I'll never forget the look on his face. He took my books and ran all the way home to his parents' house. He started screaming, 'Marcus is in trouble. Marcus is in trouble. We got to save Marcus.'"

He was instantly scared because he thought he was going to get into trouble. Creighton's parents ended up calling the police and Social Services. After this, the frequent beatings stopped, but not before Marcus tried to commit suicide by drinking bleach—"I didn't know that wouldn't work."

Although there were fewer beatings, they were more violent. At sixteen, his stepfather once again violently beat him. Marcus ran away again.

"I knew my stepfather was trying to break me, and I wouldn't be broken. The beatings were hell. I always knew I was not who they said I was. I wasn't worthless."

His family then moved to Las Vegas and left him in El Paso. Marcus ended up being sent to a foster home, the New Mexico Children's Home, where his cousin was a house parent. He thrived there on the eight-hundred-acre ranch with the other foster kids, but Marcus said it was a darker time for him. Six weeks before graduation, he was kicked out of the home for fighting and was sent to "juvie" for a couple weeks as a ward of the state.

He was released and sent to join his mother, now divorced, in Vegas. When he got there, she told Marcus to get a job and forget about going to high school. Marcus said he had to finish what he started. "She told me I was worthless, that I'd be lucky to get a GED, and to get a job and help raise my brother and sister."

They lived in a section of Las Vegas called the Baby Ghetto, the BGs: five blocks by five blocks, eighty-six homes, quadriplexes. There were almost more murders and arrests in that area than all of Las Vegas. "The school was zoned for that type of neighborhood," Marcus said.

"I walked up and saw the gang colors, seeing kids smoking weed at the stadium, and I turned on my heels and walked back home. I wanted a better school."

A mile and a half the other direction was one of the wealthiest schools. Marcus was allowed to go to that school as long as he didn't play basketball—a rule that prevented schools from poaching athletes. That was fine with Marcus.

"The first day I'm there I see kids being dropped off in Ferraris. One dad—no joke—dropped his kid off in a helicopter that landed on the football field. I'm walking with my Kmart backpack and I'm so happy."

To graduate, Marcus had to take only one academic course, biology, and the rest were electives, including computer science. He said how he and a friend, Kyle, loved the class and couldn't get enough of it. They were chewing through the textbooks.

"Two miracles happened," Marcus said. Right before Christmas, the computer science teacher said they were picking it up so fast there was nothing more he could teach them. "What I'm going to teach you is how to teach yourselves," he said. He and Kyle were to come in every day after school and ask any questions they had about the next chapter. And then they were going to teach it to the class. "I've already cleared it with the dean," his teacher told him.

Of course, their teaching the class made it into the school paper, and three months later he and a bunch of his classmates were invited to Easter dinner at his friend Carrie's house. "I had no idea how wealthy Carrie was—she never talked about it. She lived in the biggest house I've ever seen. Gated drive. Fountains. Palm trees. Perfect yard."

Then the second miracle happened. Carrie's mom, Charmaine, a beautiful woman, walked up to Marcus—the school paper with the article on him was on the kitchen counter—and said, "I hear you do computers."

Marcus said he did. She continued, "I'm going to hire you starting tomorrow. I'll pay you $20 an hour cash." He said he would be there.

"That woman changed my life," Marcus said. "She was the person that really went after what I call the poverty mentality. It's a mentality that is hard to escape. She taught me about good food and good clothes, how to tip, she taught me charisma."

During his time there, Marcus said there was a lot of crying, a lot of healing tears. And then one day Charmaine fired him.

"It's time to get a real job," she told him. Charmaine took Marcus to Burlington Coat Factory and bought him a new wardrobe. "Don't come to my house, don't come talk to me until you have a job."

So Marcus got a job at a gaming company, started a small business on the side, and moved up the ranks in the programming world. "The next thing I know I'm working for Microsoft, one of their youngest team leaders."

Marcus said it took off from there. There was a lot of stumbling, falling forward, getting fired. He learned about money management and cash flow. Successes began to accumulate. He got involved in a lot of start-ups. "If you've ever swiped your credit card at Home Depot, the reader uses a system I designed. Internationally, those systems handle $96 billion in transactions."

Marcus said he wants to paint a picture of success in programming and software for minority kids. "There are no black Bill Gates, Mark Zuckerbergs, and I've had this amazing training," he said. "You don't throw that away. Sometimes you don't think you can fly until you see someone with a cape on that looks like you."

With the success of Jammber, Marcus said we wants to shatter glass ceilings. "At first I was running from El Paso and poverty. Then I was running toward love and the family I wanted to create. But then I realized I had the opportunity to be the first black tech billionaire in history. That person still has not been made yet. If they give me much longer, I'm going to take that title."

Talk about embracing your crazy!

Creating Culture

Chris Redhage is one of my closest friends, and I can tell you first-hand he is all about creating great companies and developing meaningful relationships. As an entrepreneur, his passion is to help not only his employees but others to succeed as well. As evidence, look at the accolades his company, ProviderTrust, has earned: 2015 Best Places to Work, 10-25 employees; 2015 Healthcare Growth Company of the Year, presented by Nashville Area Chamber of Commerce and Entrepreneur Center; 2014 Small Business of the Year, Nashville Business Journal; 2012 Technology Start-up of the Year, presented by Nashville Area Chamber of Commerce and Entrepreneur Center.

His road to success has not been without setbacks, obstacles, and failure. (You might notice a common theme with just about everybody I talk about in this book—they all had experienced failures in some manner, and they had to overcome some big obstacles.) For Chris, his first challenge came in grade school.

"I couldn't read. I had a learning disability." Chris said the words on the page didn't make sense. "I would read but not comprehend." Consequently, in grade school and middle school he spent his time in a learning resource room. He took the SAT exam untimed, and in college he received extra time on tests. He said he had to learn how to learn his own way.

But his struggle with reading meant he honed his talking skills. "It was what allowed me to communicate with people. And so I've used those abilities to sell ideas and products," Chris pointed out.

In middle school, his athletic talents emerged, and people started paying attention. Ultimately, he became a Division I soccer player for the University of Richmond, where he majored in leadership studies. After graduating, he played on a number of minor league soccer teams and served as assistant coach for University of Nebraska's women's soccer team. During his time at Nebraska, the team won the Big 12 Tournament Championship, a regular season Big 12 title, and they advanced deep into the NCAA tournament.

Chris said he quit coaching and went to Louisville, Kentucky, to help a guy start companies. While he was in college, he and a team of students developed software called Connect Richmond. The software brought nonprofit organizations together to reduce duplication of services. That program is now used up and down the Eastern Seaboard. "I learned really early that I could take technology and create efficiencies."

He took that experience and, as managing partner, created three companies serving the healthcare industry. It also led to the first of two critical setbacks that would shape his future passion.

Chris recalled how on a Tuesday night he was at a Bible study being led by one of his business partners, and the next day he learned that that partner had embezzled half of a million dollars. Additionally, another business associate walked out on a $370,000 loan.

The partner was let go, but there was no getting the money back.

"I was twenty-eight at the time. I didn't know how to process my feelings—I internalized it all. It destroyed my body because of the stress," he said.

Chris said they tried to save the company. One of the entities was sold, and they were able to make another financially viable before he was able to walk away. From there, he and his new bride ended up in Nashville, where he experienced his biggest failure, though on a personal and not a business level.

In Nashville, Chris became a managing partner for a medical staffing software company. During this time, however, he had developed a lingering illness. "I had this sick feeling all the time, and no one could figure out what was wrong."

To make matters worse, Chris said his wife came home one day and said she was done with the marriage. He was caught completely off guard since they didn't have fights. "The only conflict we had was where to go to church and where to live." His wife liked their condo and didn't want to move. Ironically, after they divorced and moved, they discovered a huge mold problem behind the ceiling drywall, a result of an undetected leak, which accounted for his ongoing illness.

Chris said he thought he was doing everything to love her well, but whatever conflict his wife was experiencing wasn't brought into the open. "You do all the things that you think are the right things, and then your world falls apart," Chris said.

He said he realized that conflict, when addressed, brings you closer. When problems occurred in his marriage, he didn't have the ability to cope with them. During this time his thinking on building relationships, building trust—personal and in business—crystallized. The embezzlement and relational experiences drove him to start ProviderTrust, which offers a software service to healthcare organizations, helping them stay in compliance with regulations. "I started the company with $10,000, and six years later, we have $10 million in revenue and a valuation of $60 to $70 million."

As an entrepreneur, Chris loves that he's providing a needed and important service to the healthcare industry, but his passion is developing ethical, faithful relationships within a company. "What I wanted was people who would be with me, who wouldn't leave."

Chris said that early on he realized that talent allows you to be successful. But if you have talent and passion, you can change the world. He says they hire talented people and then fit their duties to match their talents.

"Once we get talented people, we focus on relationships. Every morning we have a ten-minute stand-up meeting. An associate talks about one of our core values, tells a story related to that value, and leads discussion," Chris said.

The values come from the ProviderTrust Playbook, which lists six core values and six core business practices. So over a month, they will have talked about each value several times. "It helps guide how people act," he said.

Whether you have an entrepreneurial spirit or not, you can still benefit from Chris's vision. You've identified your passion and written down your goals. I've talked about being different, standing out. If you want to stand out in a positive manner, take a page from the ProviderTrust Playbook. Whether you're launching a start-up, or you're working a forty-hour day job while you pursue your passion after hours, or you're working in the creative arts, the Playbook could change your world *now*. Rather than keeping his Playbook secret—the way we would in the NFL—Chris has graciously allowed me to share his plan in true mentor-like fashion. Take a look at the values listed below and imagine how this could transform a workplace, empower your coworkers or future employees, or enhance any relationship and build success in an ethical, supportive manner.

Here's the ProviderTrust Playbook:

1. Tell the truth and do what is good. Doing what is good rather than what is acceptable is essential to building trust with clients and each other. We follow through on commitments, keep our promises, and live our core values. Principle is first, and expediency at the expense of principle is not acceptable.

2. Be adventurous, creative and open-minded. It is our job to demonstrate our critical thinking, problem solving and innovation in a proactive and timely manner. Embrace adventure, change, and new ways to do things better, more efficiently, more creatively, and with ease.

3. Be the hustle you desire. There is no substitute for hard work and hustle. Always put forth additional effort to ensure we all honor commitments and exceed expectations. We strive to "wow" our teammates, our clients, and other stakeholders.

4. Help others grow and succeed. Nobody wins alone. We are a team. Developing talent is an ongoing journey with real-time feedback focused on setting people up to succeed. We develop enthusiasm in others to achieve important goals. We understand our strengths and weaknesses and want to honor both. We create paths to help all of us succeed.

5. Build open and honest relationships. Relationship is the response a person makes to other human beings. As humans, we desire to know and be known by the people we work with on a daily basis. At ProviderTrust, we desire to build authentic relationships with those around us. To accomplish this we make an effort to be open and honest in our communication, while being respectful to each other at the same time.

6. Do more with less. We approach situations with the desire to find solutions and the creativity to see new ways of achieving the right outcome. We believe opportunities are abundant and often overlooked by others. Everyone is encouraged to influence our effectiveness and efficiency by continually seeking ways to improve processes and staying focused on our individual and team goals.

Can you imagine working for a company that upheld such values? Or better, picture *yourself* leading a group of people that supported and valued each other in this manner. For that matter, these are principles that you can adapt in "running" your own life. And now that I think about it, go back and look at the people I've profiled in my "Playbook of Passionate Pursuits." You'll recognize that many of the values identified in the ProviderTrust Playbook are the same values lived out in their lives. They do what is good and right, keeping their commitments. They are adventurous—one might say "crazy"—and creative, working hard and helping others, seeking opportunities and overcoming obstacles, and they connect to people with honesty and authenticity.

Whiteboard Goals: Develop Your Playbook

Think about your passion. Which of the above Playbook values would you apply to your life to help you achieve your goals? What would you add, modify, or delete? Spend some time developing your own Playbook. Jot your ideas down—you can always amend them as you go along, as you encounter your own set of obstacles.

Here's one more tidbit about how ProviderTrust continues on their road to success. At their Monday morning meetings, everyone commits to their weekly individual and team goals. With that in mind, what one small step can you commit to today that will contribute to your success? What can you do in the upcoming week and month? Write it down.

6
THE EASY ROAD

When I finally got that call from the Carolina Panthers to say they were drafting me, a lot of people thought I had made it to the top of the world. In many ways they were right. The NFL was the best football league in the world and the best played in it. There was nowhere to go from there, and I had made it. But I didn't see it that way. I was a fifth-round pick and had my work cut out for me to even make the team, let alone to reach my goal of being the best. Even at the highest level there are those who separate themselves, becoming the best of the best.

The reason few make it to the top is because it's hard. Plain and simple. It's beyond tough. And the difficult truth is that we as humans would rather choose the easy way. Bodybuilder and eight-time Mr. Olympia Ronnie Coleman summed up "easy wishes versus hard work" with one of my favorite quotes: "Everybody wants to be a bodybuilder, but don't nobody wanna lift this heavy-ass weight."[1]

My teammates and I would sometimes say the same thing to each other in a bit more direct way: "If it was easy, everybody would do it." There is so much truth in that simple statement. It seems like human nature shares a commonality with water traveling downhill. Have you ever seen water flowing down a mountain? It's fascinating. Water doesn't take the shortest route down, it takes the easiest—the path of least resistance. Working with gravity, water twists and turns its way to the lowest point, avoiding rocks, trees, high spots, and anything else that gets in its way.

I cringe at how I have at times lived my life in a similar manner. Like many people, I've taken the easy way as opposed to the way that will get me where I want to be. Human nature is this way. So many of us will choose the easier path and settle for a lesser result. In college, it was so much easier for me to earn Bs in class than give the extra effort required to get As. I still earned my degree, but I wasn't willing to do what was necessary to be at the top of the class.

I could say I wanted an A in a particular class, but when the true cost to achieve that grade showed itself, I often settled for a lesser goal. This happens in the career lane all the time, and just as often in our personal lives. We want to be healthier, but eating right and exercising are much too difficult. It's so much easier to keep doing the same old bad habits. We want to get out of debt, but it's too slow of a process, and the sacrifice is too great. We choose the way that seems easier and, consequently, a lesser life that entails staying in debt and living paycheck to paycheck.

Time and time again we choose the easier way and the lesser goal. The price to get to the top is too steep. Why do we do this? Why are we like water? It's human nature. It's almost as simple as that. If there is an easier way to achieve the same result, most humans will take it. However, the easier way rarely ever leads to the same result. The easier way typically achieves a lesser goal. So essentially, we are talking about giving up or conceding. Sometimes I choose the hard way just to give myself a mental advantage. Knowing that I did what was more difficult gives me the upper hand over those who did not choose the more difficult path. Even if the guy next to me is more skilled, I know I can outwork and out-sacrifice him.

Climbing the Mountain

Imagine you're visiting a destination with a mountain nearby. You've heard the 360-degree view from the top is legendary and magnificent. You must get to the top to experience the view yourself. About halfway up, you realize that this is going to be much harder than you thought. The climb is steep and rocky and difficult. Your human nature swings into gear and will do its best to find an easier way. You name it: elevator, escalator, pack mule, piggyback ride? It doesn't take long for you to realize there is no easier way to the top. This steep, long, rocky path is it. So now, your human nature decides that, in fact, it doesn't need you to go to the top. It whispers, "You've seen one view, you've seen them all." In fact, it says you can survive right here. No need to climb one more difficult step. The view from here is okay. Human nature doesn't compel you to get to the top. It just needs to survive. Human nature is great. It will protect you from danger and let you know when you need something. But it will not push you to the top. That's not what it does.

So now that you're halfway to the top, you have a choice to make. Give in to your human nature and never reach the top, or find it in your heart to push on in hopes of reaching the legendary 360-degree view the top promises. We are faced with this choice time and time again throughout our lives.

The best example of people choosing the hard road is the US Marines. What it takes to become a Marine is far beyond anything I have ever done. The rigorous training and mental and physical torture they endure is awe-inspiring. Their commercial slogan, "The Few. The Proud. The Marines." is far more than mere words. These soldiers truly exemplify what it takes to get to the top. They choose the opposite of "the way of the water" and achieve greatness. It's what they endure that results in greatness. There are easier ways, but not ones that produce equal results. You may not be a Marine, but you do have the ability to achieve greatness.

The question is *how*? How do I resist my human nature and choose the hard road? A lot of you think that it's just not for you, that you weren't cut out for great things, and a mediocre life is what you're made for. Well, I emphatically disagree. You were made for greatness. Your greatness is aligned with your specific set of talents, skills, and passions. A lot of you dream dreams and set goals, but you must make sure they are for you and not somebody else. If every time you touch a plant, it dies, you may not want to set a goal to reach the top of the florist world. If you get blisters when you walk to the mailbox, running a marathon might not be your thing. Align your goals with who you are and your gifts and passions. I was big and fast and loved to hit people. Climbing to the top of the football world made sense for me. Being the largest, tallest horse jockey ever and pursuing the Triple Crown just wouldn't have been a natural path for me.

That said, there are exceptions. So many who have made it to the top have been told it was impossible because they were too dumb, short, etc. There are anomalies. A short basketball player, a mathematician who struggled in high school. Exceptions most often come when the passion to succeed far outweighs the limitations.

So let's say you are climbing the right mountain. You're following your passion and the goal is within the realm of possibility—you're still going to come to many decision points where human nature leans toward the easy road. How do you make yourself choose the hard way? There are many ways to convince your mind that it's worth it.

> **1. Accountability.** Tell the world what you want and ask them to hold you to it. As the Dominican University research study on goal setting demonstrated, this usually works best with friends and family, so find the people you respect and who aren't afraid to tell you

the truth. Peer pressure is a wonderful tool when trying to accomplish something. Having a partner is also a big help. Aligning yourself with others who want the same as you is great. There is often strength in numbers.

2. Motivation. Search for and find that thing that matters more than anything to you and use that to push or pull you in the right direction. Want to make someone proud? Hold their picture close and cling to it when the easy road calls. Want material things? Reward yourself at each benchmark of the journey. Is it pride? Is it fear that most motivates you? Use it. Assure yourself that those things that matter so much will not be achieved on the easy road. You must be convicted that the end result is worth choosing the hard way.

3. Willpower. I hate to say it, but it's true. Sometimes willpower is the only thing that can keep you from taking the easy road. Willpower. Grit. Determination. Persistence. Perseverance. Stubbornness. Intestinal fortitude. Call it what you may. These can be the most powerful characteristics helping you to stay on the hard road. Warning—they can also be the toughest. Yet when all else fails and human nature almost has its way, if you can dig down deep and by pure willpower scream, "No! I want the hard road!" that power will propel you along.

You might think, "I'm so weak! I have no willpower." But willpower, like so much else in life, is trained. Practice giving up, and you will be quick to do so. Train yourself to push past uncomfortable situations, and you won't believe the things you can achieve. Here's one willpower exercise to try: Focus on the wall in front of you and think of a flower, and only the flower, for thirty seconds. Go ahead and try it. How long did your willpower hold out before other thoughts crept in? I'll bet it wasn't too long! But the more you try to focus, the longer you can focus. When your mind drifts, simply bring yourself back to the flower. Repeat as needed. That's how willpower works. Train it to work for you rather than against you.

I consciously integrated "willpower training" into my football workouts. Inevitably, there was always a point in the workout where I wanted to quit or at least slack off. Actually, I take that back. I didn't want to quit, but my human nature wanted to take the easy way. In the case of a workout, the easy way involves putting in just enough effort to make it through without dying or looking bad to my coaches or teammates. I will admit that there are times I gave in and took the easy way. I would like to think that I quickly caught myself and jumped back into giving my best, but my willpower definitely ran out at times. I gave up fighting because I did not have the will to push any further in those moments, but I made it to the level I did by always going back for more. By going back, I was strengthening my willpower. Sometimes I gave up for five minutes and sometimes for just a quick breath, but every time I went back, my willpower grew. As my willpower grew, my endurance and muscles grew too. After a while I could dominate workouts that were once impossible for me. With a strong willpower I could push myself to the limits and see just how far I could go. This principle holds true for you also. Grow your willpower and achieve anything that you dream.

Show Me the Beef!

I recall one track practice in high school that exemplifies all three of the above principles. My coaches knew my goals were to win my track events, ultimately making me a better football player. They kept me accountable. I was motivated to be the best football player in high school, get a scholarship to college, and end up in the NFL. Sometimes, only the sheer force of will kept me going, as this story demonstrates.

It was just me and my two coaches on the track. Everyone else was finished for the year, but I was still training because I had qualified for the 100-meter and 200-meter dashes at the state track meet. My coaches were making sure I was prepared by over-training my distance, building endurance for the shorter sprints. On the agenda for that training session were four 300-meter sprints.

Three-hundred meter sprints are painful. They demand more than you want to give and push you further than you want to go. My coaches knew they were pushing me with this workout, and there was no place to hide. I was alone on the track. All eyes were on me as I hammered down my lane for the first sprint. I gave it my all. After sprint number two, I was hurting. Legs on fire, lactic acid burning through my hamstrings, sweat pouring off my brow. I wasn't feeling good. If you're familiar with this feeling, it's the one where neither standing nor sitting eases the discomfort, but only lying down in the fetal position.

After a longer than scheduled rest, I embarked on sprint number three. I was definitely fighting whatever I ate for lunch that day, but I decided to tough it out. I was grunting, running hard, giving it all that I had. I walked back to the starting line with hands locked behind my head, eyes rolled to the sky, sucking in air like my life depended on it. I looked at my coaches with a blank look on my face, and I remember Coach Kraft saying, "You about to show us your lunch?"

When you push your body past its natural limit, it has its own ways of getting you back. It was time to check what I'd had for breakfast. In fact, my lunch wanted to be part of the show too, and threatened to free itself from my stomach. I was fighting a losing battle. I urgently searched for the nearest place to deposit the contents of my stomach. Problem is, I had been running in lane one, nearest to my coaches. I thought it best not to hurl in their direction, so I lurched across the track away from them but could hold it in no longer. Soon, lanes two through seven were covered in a trail of my vomit.

As I struggled to regain composure, Coach Kraft approached, inspected the trail, and described my lunch in great detail. "Pineapple, Mandarin, and roast beef?" he queried. I nodded weakly, hoping my display of maximum effort would gain me some sympathy from him—and a shorter training session. Not so. The coaches were enjoying my pain and decided that laying it all out on the track did not mean I had nothing left. There was still one more sprint to be done. I mustered what little energy I had left and ran that last sprint like a deer that had been shot but not killed. Relief mixed with satisfaction as I dragged my weary body home. I had worked as hard as I could and knew it would pay off.

I have been analyzed and scrutinized by coaches, scouts, and fans, but I've always had an internal sense of motivation. My will to succeed has been stronger than any criticism. From an early age I knew that I had great potential but that it was up to me to develop it. The way I pushed on the track that day signifies the way I pushed myself throughout my football career. Each time a new benchmark was reached, I raised the bar. These landmarks propelled me to the highest level I could reach.

Average Is Not Okay

I don't have to be the best at everything, but having mediocre goals is unacceptable as far as I'm concerned. I can't stand the thought of being average. Nobody is made to wake up and strive to be "just okay." We are all made to excel at something. Here is my conviction: I need to be the best I can be. Not just in the things that I am good at, but in everything that I do. Anything that I give time and attention to deserves the best that I have. If it's not worth my full attention and effort, then why am I doing it? "Anything worth doing is worth doing well." Even when I am required to do things I may not want to do, I decide to give my best.

Too often we achieve well below our capabilities. Why do we allow ourselves to do this? We start out with intentions to win and then quickly find ourselves comfortable in the middle of the pack. We forget what we were running for, get distracted or even sidetracked. Maybe the cost of victory turns out to be more than we were willing to pay. Our goal may even have changed along the way, and we find ourselves running the wrong race. Whatever the cause, we have lost our drive to be the best. What are you striving for if it isn't the best? Mediocrity and complacency are best friends, and they lure us away from greatness like a soft, warm pillow from a hard day's work. The ease of mediocrity convinces us that we don't really need to be the best, but we have done enough already and doing any more would be a waste of energy.

But deep inside, we have a longing for more. Untapped potential is screaming to be found and used. We need to seek it out in ourselves and step beyond our current expectations. Sadly, if never used at all, potential will vanish, wasting away instead of flourishing. Only we can truly examine ourselves and know when we have done all that we can, but sometimes it takes someone else's point of view to uncover our untapped potential. If we don't use all that we've been given, we will never be the best we can be. Greatness is found when we explore ourselves and use each and every drop of ability we can find.

So you say, "Tim, it's impossible! How do I give my best every single time?" Fear and weakness can keep us from giving our best, but you just have to start by giving more. What if you pushed yourself harder? What if you challenged your mindset and tested your limits? There are times when I know I could have given more, and if I'm honest, I have lasting regrets about these instances. But then there are times when I'm certain I gave it all.

Examples of giving it all are my twin brothers Andrew and Peter. They may not have been the fastest or biggest guys on the field—but man, they made the most of what they were given. Drew flew around the football field, made more tackles than me, and played so hard it was written over everything he did. Pete stepped in and led us from the quarterback position with poise and confidence. They both had great high school careers, which led to the opportunity to play college football. They poured their hearts into the game, giving everything they had to maximize everything that God had given them. God didn't give them NFL abilities, but they dang sure made the most of what they had. I couldn't be more proud of my brothers for doing that.

I have seen the impact of focused willpower and the benefits of it over and over. Once you decide what you want, you must use your willpower to do whatever is necessary to achieve it. Your desire to achieve your goal must outweigh your desire for comfort or your fear of failure. In order to achieve desired results, delayed gratification and sacrifice are sometimes necessary, and willpower is the key ingredient. Although sacrifice and delayed gratification are difficult, willpower makes them possible.

These seem almost like foreign concepts these days. Is the practice/idea of sacrifice extinct? To me, sacrifice is the act of giving up something in order to gain something else. This concept can be displayed in many forms and fashions. It could look like a parent working a second job (giving up their time) so they can send their kids to a better school. A student displays sacrifice when he or she chooses to study rather than have fun with friends.

Choosing to sacrifice for future success, passing on countless opportunities for immediate pleasure, is called delayed gratification. Delayed gratification is never easy, but it is necessary to achieve goals. Many distractions come disguised as fun, so it can be difficult to see the long-term benefits of saying no now. I've had countless opportunities to choose to sacrifice in my life, and believe me, it is a choice. I chose to pursue my masters of business administration when my friends were enjoying the fun and relaxation of an NFL off-season, a decision that was not easy but has benefitted me more than I could have imagined—and is something I'm proud of to this day.

Yes, it takes extraordinary effort to take a different path. To not follow the crowd. To sacrifice something. It's that extra effort, that risk to be different, that sacrifice that leads to more, better, and unique results. It leads to special success, personal accomplishments, and deeper character developments. Both the elevator and the stairs will get you to the top of the building, but they are not equal in benefit. The easy way—the elevator—is quicker and requires less effort, while the hard way—the stairs—takes longer and is more strenuous. The elevator might seem like the obvious choice, but it may not be the best route for you. Later in the journey, the strength and character that you build on the way up the stairs will give you the endurance you need to complete your path. When evaluating options, weighing the long-term benefits versus the short-term gratification will guide your decisions toward wisdom rather than immediate satisfaction. When you choose the fast way over the scenic route, you sacrifice the beauty of the journey. When you read the CliffsNotes instead of the novel, you sacrifice the depth of description in the story. Every choice has a consequence.

Below Par

I do recall one of the times that I made the wrong choice. Coach McKendry and I had been friends a long time. We grew up together and played high school football and basketball together. Being a couple of years older, he had graduated and joined the Trojan football staff as a JV assistant. I was learning how to navigate the "friend-turned-coach" relationship. One summer day before my senior year, we went golfing. Summer football workouts were optional. And by optional, I mean mandatory. And by mandatory, I mean if you missed one, it would be forever held against you and may God have mercy on your soul. You see, football coaches have a special way of instilling commitment and accountability! Our Trojan squad had three days a week of lifting with speed drills beforehand. Strictly optional (cough, cough), of course. Now I would never in my high school life miss a weight room session. After all,

I loved having muscles, but that speed session didn't seem so necessary. Let's be honest, I was plenty fast, and I hadn't met a football player who could catch me. So the round of golf was taking longer than we wanted. If we chose to finish it, we would surely miss the speed work. I remember the decision point clearly. Sacrifice the remainder of my golf round to make it to speed drills, or finish the round and skip the drills? I made the choice: we would finish the round and miss speed work. No big deal. I was playing great golf (probably not), I was a senior captain who never missed anything, and I was with a coach (buddy)! I had my chance and I made my choice.

I got back for the weightlifting session, and during the stretch before the lift, my main goal was to avoid eye contact with Coach Hudkins (guilty much?). As the stretch ended and guys filed from the hallway to the weight room, Hudkins called me over. "Where were you?"

"Golfing," I answered, embarrassed.

"I don't give a #*@! if you were playing in the US Open, get your ass here!"

"Yes, sir."

And that was it. He could have said a lot more, but I think he knew that I knew if it was okay for me to miss, it was okay for others to miss. If I didn't sacrifice, then why would anybody else?

I had made a conscious choice not to sacrifice. That sinking feeling following that choice has stayed in my memory and led me to make many more decisions to sacrifice in my life. Every sacrifice has an attached cost, good or bad.

Perhaps I can thank my parents, once again, for teaching me about making choices and understanding the benefits of sacrifice. Each of us boys were given a weekly allowance. The allowance was determined by the expected costs we would face for the year: new shoes, school clothes, supplies, birthday gifts, personal spending, etc. That yearly cost would be divided by 52, and that determined our weekly allowance. As a kid, I wanted a bike, so I saved and saved my allowance until I had enough money for that BMX Dyno Comp with the 360-degree gyro-style handlebars. I could have bought tons of stuff in the meantime, but I made the choice to delay my gratification for something bigger. Do we do that as grown-ups, or do we just put that big television on the credit card? If we are in debt, do we find extra work, not take those trips with those extra luxuries we would like? Or do we take the easy way and borrow more? Sacrifice is hard! It sucks to give up what you want. It's not fun to go without, to miss out, or to be the only one working so hard or doing the right thing. But so what! It's worth it. I promise. Twelve-year-old Timmy enjoyed and took care of that bike way more than he would have if Dad had just given it to him. And so will you, with that house or car or that paid-off credit card. When you get that raise or award, it's so worth it because you know the sacrifice it took to achieve it.

Being drafted into the NFL was one of those things for me. Regardless of anything else, it was the sacrifice that only I truly knew, that made that accomplishment so special and made all the sacrifice worth it.

So I ask you, is there more you can do? What if you pushed yourself and tested the limits? What if you actually took off your preconceived notions of "I can't" or "I won't" or "I shouldn't" and found your real limits? Give it a try. Say to yourself, "I'm going to go as hard as I can for as long as I can." Then evaluate once you're done and next time go harder, further. I guarantee you'll achieve things that you never thought possible. We limit ourselves before we even begin. That's where the great people separate themselves. They take those limits off, they train more, study more. It's the mindset of a champion to believe they can succeed despite all circumstances. What if you pushed that far? What could you accomplish? Who could you impact?

It's exciting to think about the limitlessness we can have if we throw off the restrictions. There are endless possibilities if you allow yourself the freedom to explore. To maximize your gifts and abilities you must remove the limitations. I know there is fear that you'll discover something you can't handle. But you'll have to face your fears along the way. It's a beautiful thing to face those fears and overcome them.

Whiteboard Goals: Picture Your Motivation

What can you do to help you choose the hard road over the easy road? For me, as you know, I kept my whiteboard with my goals always in front of me. Another way is to picture what a life of success looks like. Create a vision board. For example, if your goal is to make an impact through foreign mission work, you tack a picture to your board of that young orphan boy you met on your last trip to Africa, reminding you of why you're on the hard road. Or you might pin motivational sayings to the board urging you onward. Post pictures of people who have accomplished the same thing you're after. Or draw your own illustration of the book you want to write, the album you want to cut, or the diploma you want to earn. In other words, find photos, sayings, artwork, or anything else that reminds you of why you're making your sacrifices and put them on your board for daily motivation.

FLIP OFF FATE

7
SLAP ME UPSIDE THE HEAD

I swear the complaining never stopped. At lunch they would complain about the workout they just had or were about to have. Before practice, they were dreading the schedule they'd been given or the dress code. It didn't matter what it was, they complained about it. And I'd had enough. I couldn't take any more. I did what I always did; I made a positive comment. They laughed at me for undermining their negativity.

"Heaven forbid someone say something positive," I responded to their laughing.

For a long time, it would be a phrase that I would be known for. Mostly because my locker neighbors, good friends at Penn State, and chief complainers—Steve Roach, Robert Price, and BranDon Snow—repeated it for years. They knew I loved them, but that I wasn't going to pass up a chance to give them a hard time. As annoying as it was, I was proud of it because if only for a moment, those guys were reminded of an alternative to complaining.

It's not uncommon. We tend to see the bad instead of the good. It's a tool we use to get through something unpleasant. You will find it around job sites, offices, and sports teams alike. Misery loves company. So let's talk about our boss, the rules, and the nonsensical things we have to do for no good reason. I mean, it won't change if we do it or not, but it might make us feel better or somehow make the misery or monotony go by faster. I've done it too. Given in to the urge to gripe. Did it help? No, not really.

There's a problem with this human habit. No good comes from it. It doesn't work. Nothing changes about the circumstances. It doesn't go away. All it does is bring negativity. And that is never a good thing. And what you put out into the world will come back to you. What you think about and talk about will come about. Putting out good vibes and energy? They will come back. Negative words and emotions flowing from you? You will see them return. I don't know what or when it happened, but somewhere along the line, I realized the power of positive thinking. I bought into the idea that what I say and think actually has an impact on what happens in my life.

Looking back, I see this principle working so clearly. Can you see it in your own life? What you think about, you will likely talk about. What you talk about you will likely do. Therefore, what you think about, you will likely do. It's simple math really. If a = b, and b = c, then a = c.

Take a minute and take stock of what you're putting into your head all day long. If you're immersed in positive ideas that come from such things as motivational books, spiritual thoughts, TED talks, and community service, your actions will take on a sheen of positivity. But if you're loading your mind up with negative content such as gossip, criticism, talk radio, and snarky social media, you will likely carry that negativity into your actions.

Said differently, what you put in determines what comes out. Garbage in. Garbage out. You are what you eat. Reap what you sow. As a man thinks, so he is. What goes up must come down (oh wait, that's gravity!). There are a million ways to say it, but it all means the same thing.

"Whether you believe you can do a thing or not, you are right." This quote, attributed to Henry Ford in 1947, says it best. Have you ever thought you couldn't do something, maybe even said it out loud, and then proven yourself right? I have. "Oh, I'm terrible at spelling." And then you fail a spelling test. "I'll never be able to hit a curveball." Then striiiiike! "I might miss this putt." You just did. "I won't get the promotion." Sure enough, you don't. The power of the mind. You thought it. Then your body acted out what the brain and mouth commanded.

It works the other way too. Tell yourself that nothing will keep you from your goal and nothing will. Think the girl will say yes when you ask her out and ... it might take a few tries ... but she will come around! The positive mind is so powerful. You hear stories of unbelievable events that would have never happened were it not for some crazy individual who had the gumption to believe it could be done. Swimming the English Channel, climbing Mt. Everest, running the first sub-four-minute mile. Take Arnold Schwarzenegger as just one example. Seemingly everything he set his mind to achieve, he did.

He was born in Austria to a working-class family. His father was a policeman who, Schwarzenegger said, physically abused him. In his early teen years, he saw bodybuilding as a way to achieve success. He trained relentlessly, becoming Mr. Universe at the age of twenty—the youngest ever. As prestigious as that award was, he wanted to become the greatest bodybuilder in the world, an honor that went to Mr. Olympia. At the age of twenty-three, he won the Mr. Olympia competition, also the youngest ever to do so. He went on to win seven Mr. Olympia titles. But of course, Schwarzenegger didn't stop with being the world's top bodybuilder. He became a film star, winning a Golden Globe for New Male Star of the Year, playing opposite Sally Field in *Stay Hungry.* He became a top box-office draw, and his films have grossed more than $3 billion worldwide. He graduated with a degree from the University of Wisconsin and became a US citizen. He overcame his Austrian birth and accent to be elected to the top post in California, twice serving as governor.[1] Most people growing up in Schwarzenegger's shoes would have thought such achievements were impossible. What I want you to see here is his attitude. He didn't succeed because he was the strongest, smartest, or best actor, or most gifted politician, but because his positive attitude and belief in himself led to unbelievable success along every avenue he chose to pursue.

We limit ourselves all the time. We tell ourselves that we can't do something and never will. We convince ourselves that we aren't good at something. We believe the label someone else puts on us. Then we proceed to live that out. "I'm not smart enough to go to college." So you walk that out. You don't study hard enough to reach your full potential. You don't do the extra work. You don't try your hardest. You don't get the extra tutoring. So you prove yourself right. You don't get into college. "I'll never get a promotion. They don't like me. It's not fair." And you live your life at the office under this self-proclaimed label. You don't do the best work you can do because you believe it won't matter. You don't take advantage of opportunities that come up because you believe it won't help. You don't volunteer or apply for promotions because you believe you'll get shut down, and you end up living out what you've claimed for yourself.

Label Liberation

Throughout my pro career a lot of people tried to limit me. I was labeled a "Special Teams Ace" and a "Career Special Teamer." What that label really meant was "not a starter." It meant, "We think you are great at special teams, but not good enough to be our starting linebacker." That label was put on me by coaches, general managers, teammates, and the media. It was a label that I certainly did not like and never let define me. I always wanted more. I always wanted to be a starter and knew that I had the capability to be one if given the opportunity. I always worked, studied, and practiced as if I were a starter, waiting for that opportunity. Always hoping, wishing, and ready for that chance.

If I had bought into the labels and identified myself with that "not a starter/never a starter" label, I could have just settled into my role, given up my goal, and accepted the fact that I would never start. In that case, I would have always have been a career special teamer and, in my mind, never reached my full potential. Just because someone doesn't promote you doesn't mean you're not promotable. Just because someone doesn't view you a certain way doesn't mean that you have to act the way that they view you.

I always planned on being a starter. And even though a lot of times I was just trying to survive in the NFL, I was always working and preparing and wanting to be a starter. Never limiting myself as "just" a special teams player. I always prepared mentally to play defense, knowing the playbook and game plan each week, even without the practice reps of a starter. It took me four years, but I finally got on the field to play defense. The Titans finally gave me a chance, and I took full advantage of it. Now, I wasn't a starter yet, but it was a step in the right direction. They put me on defense in situations when we needed an extra linebacker. I would come in and play a few downs a game, and I would make a big play here, a big play there, a nice tackle here. I proved myself reliable. Next thing you know, the next season I was backing up all three linebacker spots. Somebody would go down inside; I would jump in to play middle linebacker.

Somebody would go down outside; I would play outside linebacker. And I proved myself reliable there.

Now I was still playing special teams, my main role and responsibility, but I viewed myself as more. I didn't limit myself. And then it happened. Eventually, somebody got hurt and, "Tim, you're going to be the starter." Even if in everyone else's minds I was still a special teamer, I knew I was their best option to be the starter. This was my opportunity to prove to everyone that the labels were wrong—I wasn't a career special teamer. I could play defense and rise above all those low expectations and limitations that had been put on me.

One of the biggest compliments I got as a professional football player was when I ended up starting the last five or six games of the 2012 season, and the linebacker coach told me that I came in and did such a good job that they didn't miss the starter whom I had replaced. And that confirmed in my mind what I had been working for and believing my whole career, that I *could* do it, that I *did* have the skills and the ability and the work ethic and the leadership. All those things paid off because I proved that I could be a starter in the NFL. I didn't let the limitations that others tried to put on me define me. And therefore I didn't limit myself. If I had given in and settled for less, I would not have been ready when the opportunity presented itself.

A lot of times that's what we do. We hear our given labels and become aware of how we are seen and then we claim those views as our own. Really, what we're doing is putting a ceiling on our potential and limiting ourselves from reaching our best self. There are a thousand excuses why we can't do something. And we can accept those excuses that limit us from excelling, or we can do what a local group of Nashville high school students did and achieve unexpected success.

Maplewood High School is located in a "dangerous" neighborhood in East Nashville, but a group of students didn't let that hold them back. These students joined a chess team coached by a volunteer, Armin Begtrup, at the Martha O'Bryan Center, an anti-poverty nonprofit located in the same area.

The story about the chess team members ran in the *The Tennessean.* Maplewood High was known more for athletic success than academic success. The hood, thugs, delinquents—it's how the neighborhood was viewed; it's how they were viewed, according to Begtrup. Of course, the students do have challenges. At least one member, according to the story, was homeless, moving from place to place every week. And when the chess team was formed at the beginning of the year, none of them knew how to play chess.

So what did they do? In tournaments, they won three first-place trophies. And out of sixty-seven teams, they were one of four that qualified for state and regional competitions against some of the highest achieving private and public schools, against students who had played chess their whole lives and memorized many of the game's classic gambits. The coach said they didn't have time to learn all that. They used basic strategies and made unconventional moves that caught opponents off guard. The coach said, "Their self-worth has skyrocketed."

When the reporter asked the students if they thought they were the underdogs, in a chorus they replied, "No." These young scholars rejected the labels that had been put on them.[2]

When people live up to whatever they've been labeled, positive or negative, it's called a self-fulfilling prophecy. It's also called expectancy-confirming bias. There's a famous study done by two researchers, Rosenthal and Jacobson, in 1968, demonstrating this. The research, called the Pygmalion study, measured the success of students based on teacher expectations. The teachers were convinced by the researchers that some of their students had been determined to be late bloomers, and the teachers should expect great progress for those students during the year. The reality was that the students were chosen at random and labeled as late bloomers. The result? Those designated as late-bloomers gained more in IQ than other students. The teachers' expectations were self-fulfilling. Later studies have also shown that negative expectations—those that undermine students' achievements—were more powerful than positive expectations.[3]

Imagine if we told ourselves that negative labels would not limit us. Imagine if you were convinced that the only limitation you had was the span of your life, and anything you wanted to achieve before you die, you could. What would you accomplish? Where would you go? What would you do? I claim you would do unbelievable things. You would do incredible things. What if you saw the mountain peak and you said, "I'm going to climb it!" Then all you did was reach the peak. Time is my only limitation, but I have enough heart, desire, and will to keep climbing!" What's that mountain peak for you? Is it a job title? Is it respect in your field? Is it a certain position of wealth or success? Is it a number of people you want to impact through service? Is it a mindset of peace? Whatever that is, just keep climbing. Just keep going. Don't let anything but time stop you. When we convince ourselves and take those limitations off, the sky really is the limit. Only you can determine how far you'll go, or how far you won't.

Two Accounts

One of the reasons our minds are so powerful is because we understand and remember what's happened in the past. This can be both positive and negative. And it can be both helpful and hurtful. If I remember that somebody once tried some activity or to reach some goal and failed, it could keep me from trying. But if I remember that somebody has done it before me, then I might believe I can do it. It works both ways. And here is where the mind is so powerful: You can build up those memories for yourself over time. The more and more victories you have, the more and more success stories you have, the more successes you believe you'll have in the future.

Let's put it this way. Throughout your life you have two accounts. Every time you make a good decision, you make a deposit in the "I'm awesome" account. Every time you make a bad decision, you get a deposit in the "Slap me upside the head" account. If you keep making one good decision followed by one bad one, they're cancelling each other out. But if you deposit two or three in a row in the "Awesome" account, now you're building momentum. You're building positive memories, habits in your mind. And you're proving to yourself that you can. Now let's take the "I'm awesome" account and call it "not quitting" or "doing one more" or "going a little extra," or call it "winning." Now, every time you accomplish one of these, the account grows, as does your confidence.

Don't get me wrong. There's going to be "Slap me upside the head" deposits along the way, but fewer and fewer as your good decisions compound. We build success one step here, one little thing there. Our minds are so powerful that we remember those and we tell ourselves, "Oh, yeah! Remember when I did this." So we get to a tough point where we want to quit, to give in and stop fighting. Our brain says, "We have been here before and look, we have a whole account full of 'I'm awesome' deposits from good choices we made, from times we wanted to quit but didn't. Times when we did quit, but got back up and kept fighting— and the results showed it worthwhile." Our minds allow us to push further. They allow us to do more. They allow us to keep going. It's that account full of decisions, successes, and memories of things that we've done that will push us when new tests present themselves.

This is how we reach new heights. When we get to a point where we want to quit, we can look into the "I'm awesome" account and push a little further. Now we might not make it all the way to the top that day, but we pushed a little further than before.

So what do you do when you're looking at your accounts and your "Slap me upside the head" account has a far greater balance than your "I'm awesome" account? When your bad decisions have far outweighed your good ones, and your losses far outweigh your wins, then it can be hard to get on the right track. When you get to those tough points, you look at your accounts and say, "I couldn't do it before, I can't do it now." And, "I quit last time, I'm going to quit this time." What do you do when drawing on your past record only promotes more defeat?

Well, I encourage you with this: it only takes one right choice to get started in the direction you want to go, so make one decision right now. Win once. Then win again. Make one good decision. Then make another. Convince yourself that you can make one good decision. And then cash that decision in the "I'm awesome" account. That positive accomplishment leads to more positive accomplishments, and your mind says, "I can do one more." Don't see it as a mountain. Think of the punchline to the question, "How do you eat an elephant?" The answer, of course, is one bite at a time. One bite, one choice, one step at a time will get you where you want to go.

Remove those self-imposed limitations. Build those "I'm awesome" habits. You'll realize that you can accomplish anything—you're only limited by your time on earth.

Belief and Action

Now let's delve into this a bit deeper and look at some practical implications. I've talked about *belief* and *action*. If belief is step one, then action is step two. One does not work without the other. You need to believe. In order for your belief to mean anything, you have to put action behind it. In order for your action to mean anything, it's got to have belief behind it. I can sit here and tell you I believe that I will pass this math test. Closing my eyes, I repeat, "I believe, I believe, I believe." I show up for the math test and I fail. Well, why did that happen? It happened because I believed but didn't do anything about it.

See, what I really mean when I say "I believe I will pass this math test" is that I believe in my ability to prepare and perform when it's test time. That belief must move me to action. I study. I practice. And the test comes, and I'm ready. I pass the test because my belief led me to action.

That applies to everything in life. Belief must move us to action. In the Bible, James makes a similar point: "So it is with faith: if it is alone and includes no actions, then it is dead" (James 2:17, paraphrase). Don't tell me what you believe, *show me*! The sign that you truly believe is action. You cannot just believe. You have to *do*. What good is a football team that simply thinks about all the things that they're going to do on the field, all the great plays they're going to make, all the wonderful football games they believe they'll win, but they don't practice or train? When game time comes, those great plays don't happen and the wins don't come if they haven't worked for it, if they haven't practiced. They haven't put their belief into action.

The Iowa State football coach had it right. Before their game in 1940 with arch rival Nebraska, he wrote this on the chalkboard:

"If you think you can, you can; if you think you can't, you're right."

That was seven years before Henry Ford made his famous comments about believing you can![4] (A philosopher-coach. Who would have thought?) I have met so many people in my life that just talk, talk, talk. It's like, "Man, would you just shut up and show me!" If all he or she does is talk all day, I have no respect for that person. But people who walk the walk, go out, and do exactly what they said they were going to do? I respect them. I respect individuals who show you what they are all about, rather than tell you. They believe who they are, and they go out and prove it. No doubt there is a time and place for trash talk, but you'd better back it up.

It's a beautiful thing when belief moves us to action. It's awesome to see somebody who believes in themselves so much that they continue to try, continue to work, continue to hone their craft, continue to put in the hours, put in the time and the effort—physically and mentally—to prove themselves right. If you're not doing the same, then I have to ask, do you really believe in what you're saying?

Positive Intent

So many great things have come about because of someone's belief. Things that never would have happened otherwise. On the other hand, have you ever seen someone just doing, doing, doing? Always busy. Always working so hard, you're wondering, "Why are they doing that? What are they working for?" When you ask them, they say they don't know, or it seemed like the thing to do, or they didn't know what else to do. They have no compelling belief behind what they're doing. They're just working to work. They're just busy to stay busy. Action is really pointless if it doesn't have reason, belief, behind it. Maybe this is you. Maybe you fell into a job and got comfortable. Maybe you've never asked yourself what you really want, or maybe you think this is the best you can do. But I believe you are called to live a life of meaning.

Believing doesn't make something so, and doing doesn't make something worthwhile. But when you believe and you do? Great things can be accomplished. It's the mind's ability to move the body into action that is one of its greatest sources of power. Or one of its greatest displays of power.

Positive thinking in action. We all have countless opportunities throughout our day, throughout our life to choose positive or to choose negative. When you wake up and see it raining outside, do you choose to let that ruin your day, or do you give thanks for having a good umbrella? Is a fluctuating stock market an opportunity or a disaster? If your boss gets promoted, do you expect the new boss to be difficult, or do you see it as an opportunity to demonstrate your talents? We always have a choice. We have a choice to be a pessimist or an optimist. Glass half full, glass half empty. Which one are you? I believe that a positive mindset produces positive results more often than not.

I've often seen this kind of thinking on display. For example, two athletes the same size with the same strength are working out. They both get on a bench press with the same exact weight on it. One pumps himself up with positive talk before he attempts the lift: "I can. I will. I got this. I'm strong enough." The second person says to himself, "I probably won't. I might fail. I'm not sure. That looks heavy. I don't know if I can do this. I don't know if I can lift this." They both get under the barbell, and the one with the positive thoughts will get it done. The one with the negative thoughts will not get it done. The mind is so powerful that the one has convinced himself that he can and the other has convinced himself that he can't, even though both athletes have the same physical capability. The one's mind brought him to a higher level physically than the other one could.

I'm not talking about unrealistic things. I'm not talking about magical experiences or magical feats of jumping great distances or winning amazing contests because you believe and say that you can. I'm talking about taking your capabilities to their limit, to their maximum potential because of the power of your mind. I'm talking about positive thoughts pushing you to a new level.

Whiteboard Goals: Audit Your Account

Take a few minutes to audit your "I'm awesome" account. In other words, recall and write down five success stories. Maybe it was that tight deadline you met against all odds. Or something simple—but an important accomplishment— such as passing up that extra dessert so you could meet your calorie goal. Perhaps you hit it out of the park with a great presentation. Or you ran an extra mile on the treadmill. Whatever your victories were, big or small, write them down to remind yourself that you can accomplish what you put your mind to. Then act to add another deposit to your "I'm awesome" account.

8
IN CONTROL
OF JOY

Here's a secret—well, more like a truth that we constantly seem to forget: Understanding what we control (and accepting what we don't control) leads to a freedom of mind. And that freedom allows a spirit of joy and peace—rest—to enter your life.

Admitting what is in your control and what isn't can be difficult. In football, I could control what I knew from the playbook and watching game film, how hard I worked, my attitude, my daily living choices. But there was so much I couldn't control. I couldn't put myself in the game; that was the coach's decision. I couldn't control what the other players did. All I could control was me and how I reacted to what happened around me.

Here's a great example of controlling what can be controlled.

After signing my letter of commitment to Penn State, sometime in the spring, I received a fully detailed workout packet from the Penn State football strength staff. Even though it looked like it hadn't been updated in twenty years, I thought, "If this is what the college guys are doing to train for the season, then so will I. I'm one of them." So I decided I would follow that packet as best I could, including daily lifting and running exercises. Sometimes the packet would say, "Monday—run three miles." On Wednesday it would say, "Run four miles." It had these long-distance runs in there.

I'm not scared of a good run, so I would go ahead and set out on what, for me, were long-distance runs. I would head to the high school track and run four miles, three miles, or whatever was indicated that day in between the lifting, sprints, and position-specific drills. I thought it amazing how much distance training these guys would do in the off-season. But I couldn't control what the old blue workout manual said, only what I did and how hard I went. I could have just as easily decided that I didn't need to run like this, but I proceeded to do this throughout the summer. I also chose to go to Penn State that summer prior to our fall camp. I got there in July and spent a couple weeks working out with the team.

One morning, they had what they called The 20-Minute Test. The test was held down on the track, and you had twenty minutes to just run as far as you could. Different positions had different standards for how far they had to run. The group I was running with, the running backs, ran in lane eight. It was a big collegiate track, and I'm thinking, "Hey, I'm ready for this. I've been running all summer. I'm sure these guys have too, of course. I'm in the best running shape of my life. I feel like I'm ready for the track team, let alone the football team."

So we start the run. I take off at a very fast pace, which I'd been doing. I mean, I'm used to this. Around lap two or so, I start getting some looks from some older guys and start getting comments as I pass them on the track.

"Hey, man, you know this is twenty minutes, right?"

Or another would call out, "Hey, dude, you might want to pace yourself."

"You might want to take it easy."

I didn't say this, of course, but I'm thinking, "What are you guys talking about? We're running for twenty minutes. I've been doing this. I can run three miles in twenty minutes— maybe even three and a half." I'm just flying.

Over the next four years I would find out that nobody— and I do mean nobody—had been running as much as I had that summer. In fact, instead of the numerous long-distance runs listed in the outdated workout packet, maybe once a week the guys would run a few miles around campus. That was it for distance. I ended up running almost twelve laps in twenty minutes in those outside lanes, setting for myself a standard of work at Penn State. I think that's a perfect example of controlling what you can and not worrying about the rest.

Now, you want to be a long-distance runner? Run long distances. You want to improve your jump shot? Shoot jump shots. You want to be a better writer? Put time in learning how to write and practice writing. Most things are not secret; they're not complicated. They require time. They require attention. They require doing.

As I said, admitting what is or isn't in your control is a freeing thing. It frees your mind to not only spend its power on what it can affect, but to enjoy life knowing you've done what you can. This opens the door to living in the moment and experiencing joy.

Because I had done my preparation, worked hard at practices, and controlled those elements I could control, I found it easy to let joy spread over me during our games. Those memories are so vivid—probably because it happened so many times, almost every Sunday afternoon in the fall for seven years. During a timeout, typically for a television advertising break, I'd be bopping to some hip hop beat blaring through the stadium speakers. Bouncing somewhere around the 30-yard line as my team prepared to kick off, I would head butt a teammate, our face masks clashing. Then I would jump up and down to make sure my muscles were as loose as a cheetah's. All part of my pre-strike routine. I would take one last glance at my team and the crowd, and then it would happen. The anticipation would build throughout the stadium, and a big stupid grin would spread across my face.

"This is what we get to do today?!" I would ask out loud, directed as much at God and myself as anybody else. I found joy in that moment. Each and every time. And then I would go wild and show the opponent's ball carrier how joyous I was.

You say, "Of course, you found joy on an NFL field. You were living your dream!"

I hear you. I definitely hear you. But here's another secret: not everyone found joy on the NFL field. A lot of guys found stress, pressure, and anxiety. Joy is found when you look for it. By doing what you need to do, and taking care of what you can control, you leave room for joy to show itself. Joy has trouble showing up when bad attitudes are dominant—an attitude that results from such things as anger, resentment, or jealousy. An attitude that comes from worrying about what you can't control—when you think the quarterback is not throwing enough passes your way, or you're not getting enough opportunities, or your team isn't paying you as much as the guy that's in the locker next to you, or the coaches are paying too much (or too little) attention to you. These bad attitudes, unfortunately, can affect others.

Make Joy

I find joy all over the place. Some might even say I make joy. The way I see it, life is what you make it, so I try to make joy. I even control the possibility of joy by scheduling it into my life. That's right. I make sure to plan things that will help bring me joy. One of those things is traveling. I love to travel and when I do, it's always to see someone I love or with someone I love.

One of my favorite trips each year is Brocation. Brocation is the Shaw brothers' annual vacation, a tradition we started when my oldest brother started having kids. It's our intentional time together, no wives, work, or kids. It is a trip to just be with each other. The four of us go somewhere warm for a long weekend, and we eat, play golf, swim, and relax. It matters to us, so we make time for it, budget for it, and make it happen. It brings us joy.

I find joy in simple things like a round of golf or a good book. My love affair with golf took off during my summers at Penn State. I would work out first thing in the morning, go to a class or two, and then head to the Blue-White Golf Course. I didn't have any money and golf isn't cheap, so I used my brain. I got a job working maintenance at the course! I only took the job to pay for my golfing habit, and the job came with free golf benefits. So needless to say, I spent more time playing golf than I did working.

Golfing was the opposite of football for me and was my favorite way to relax. I always took out a golf cart, as golf is not my idea of exercise. I love the natural beauty of a golf course, and it's a great way to spend time outside on a nice day. Maybe the best part is that you are with friends. It's just a great activity. I'm with fun people on a nice day, relaxing and playing a competitive game all at the same time. It's easy for me to find joy in that. Throughout my life, golf has also been a gateway allowing me to meet new people, connect with them, and bring others together.

On the opposite end of the spectrum, I've found a lot of joy in reading, though much less of a social activity. Reading is an opportunity to learn something, expand your thinking, be challenged, motivated or convicted, or to escape reality. I can't begin to explain how much reading has added value to my life. Whether it's deep study in the Bible, or a light story about a fictional monk, the wisdom I have gained is priceless. I love learning from other people's lives, and reading is a great way to do that. More than anything, the benefit comes from admitting that I don't know everything, quieting myself, and seeking a different view. There is joy for me in reading.

Another constant ingredient in finding joy, no matter my life situation, is having a sense of humor. I laugh a lot. I'm goofy from time to time. I'm serious when I need to be, usually, but laughter is a must for me. Has it gotten me into trouble? On more than one ... hundred occasions, yes. But I swear I have it under control for the most part now. In seventh grade, I thought it would be funny to tear away one guy's "tear-away" pants, the kind with buttons up both sides. As I ran down the hallway with his pants in hand, the whole school simultaneously found out that he was only wearing boxers underneath. In second grade, when our substitute teacher walked in with a grey beehive hairdo, I started yelling, "Witch! Witch!" She did not appreciate the humor, and neither did my parents when they were informed of my actions. I grew up, adjusted and tweaked my comedic timing through the help of friends and family, not to mention many disgruntled ex-girlfriends (they just didn't "get me"), intentionally looking for the humor in every situation. The point is, I am determined to have a good time and not take life so seriously. Those of you who don't find things so funny might say, "That's just not my sense of humor. It's not the way I am." You don't have to be born with a certain sense of humor to laugh at something like my corny jokes (I love Reader's Digest jokes), but you could adjust your mindset to see the lighter side of life.

Crack Yourself Up

To find the humor in life, like I do, you have to look for it. You have to set your mind to the fact that things go wrong and annoying things happen, but life goes on. And it goes on a lot more smoothly if you can laugh. Be serious when it benefits you, but chill out when it doesn't. Flat tire? Stuff happens. Call that girl you like by the wrong name? Hopefully, she reads this chapter, too, and figures it will make for a great story someday. Throw your computer out the window? Wait—that one is all on you. Life is full of stuff that you can't control, so it's best to control your reaction to that stuff. And laughter is a great reaction.

I've been through some tough and bad situation in my life, but nothing has compared to living with ALS. I'm so thankful that as my body may struggle, my humorous outlook does not. I am determined to laugh through the hard times in life. Yes, there are times when I cry, scream in anger, and just flat out struggle. There are times for those things in life. Don't cover or deflect those things with humor, but when those things happen, allow yourself to smile and laugh anyway.

Doggone Funny!

As my physical strength lessens and my balance wavers, I have begun to fall more frequently than I like to admit.

Me, the former professional athlete. I struggle to get down a step or walk through a doorway. I have fallen in a variety of places, some more fun than others. At home (carpet is a bonus). Outside (concrete is no fun). On a plane (not super fun, but an audience is a bonus). And on a golf course (fairways are more fun than bunkers!). Each time I've managed to laugh, even through blood and stitches. At times I've had someone there to share the laugh, other times I've laughed alone. A laugh is always better when you can share it. I've scared people around me when I've fallen, but it's not their fault. They don't know how much I miss the contact of sports. I'm sure that my laughter has eased their worry.

One time I was leaving someone's house after a meeting, and after slowly wobbling down the three big steps that led from the house to the driveway, I turned around and realized the people at the meeting were watching me the whole time, probably holding their breaths. "Don't worry," I said, with a smile on my face. "I'm a much better driver than walker!" Laughter makes everything better.

Another thing that is happening to me as a result of ALS is my speech becoming more slurred. Sloppy speech coupled with the clumsy walk only leads people who don't know me to think one thing: "He must be drunk!" Ha! I can't blame these people because I know how I look and sound. I would make the same assumption if I were them. As incredibly frustrating as this is, I have to laugh every time someone makes a comment. The alternative is being angry and correcting them—to no good end. So I choose to laugh at them and myself instead, and have another drink.

One odd symptom of ALS is possible loss of emotional control. In some, it manifests in uncontrolled crying. Thank God, for me, it shows up in uncontrollable laughter. I kid you not, I take a pill to help me control my mouth. Now that's funny in itself! Seriously, if someone tells a joke, the group would naturally start laughing, and the group would then naturally stop laughing. But I don't stop; I just keep on laughing. It can be awkward. A serious conversation to be had? I'm probably going to bust out laughing when it's inappropriate. I laughed uproariously when my friend told me her dog had died. (Thankfully, she thought it was funny that I was laughing and ended up joining me.) If I'm eating or drinking, look out, because particles will fly. Best not to be funny during meal times. What a great symptom to have! If you had to pick a symptom, that would be it. It also gives me an excuse to be my goofy self.

They say laughter is the best medicine, and I agree. If I can laugh through this torturous disease, I'm pretty sure that you can laugh through your circumstances. Laughter does not diminish the relevance of your problem, but it does help your perspective. If you can recognize that a lot of life is out of your control and that the way you react is a huge factor in how things turn out, you will handle life's trials with less difficulty. There is joy to be found in the hard times, and there are people to share that joy with. The more people you can laugh with, the more joy you will find.

Facing the reality of my diagnosis meant admitting the likelihood of major physical decline. As tough as this was, and still is, to wrap my head around, it is necessary for my mental health. At one point I told my Dad that if I wind up in a wheelchair, then I want him to push me fast. So what if I tip over and get banged up. At least I will know I'm alive.

I could choose to live in a bubble as safe and protected as possible, but to me, that's the same as dying. I choose to live with the danger of hurt and tragedy out in the unprotected world. One way I do this is by continuing to play golf, even as I struggle to get around the course. To me, it's living.

Chuck and I have become good friends all because of golf. We are both retired, albeit forty years apart, and therefore free to golf every day. Chuck quickly accepted the thankless job of chauffeuring me around the course, and I took the job of regularly taking his money in our three-dollar game. The added pressure that Chuck has is taking care of me during the round. I keep him on his toes with the occasional fall, stumble, or drop of the club. All part of my victory plan. On number 14 at the Golf Club of Tennessee, Chuck hit a poor tee shot and decided to hit another from there (that's three, Chuck). I grabbed a ball and got out of the cart. The momentum from my toss leaned my body forward, too forward for my already confused equilibrium. The slight effort I made to correct my balance was thwarted by the 10-inch-high wooden rail separating the cart path and the knee-high grass, and so … down I went. I knew my weakening arms couldn't catch me, so I just braced for contact and enjoyed the trip down.

I shared the contact between face, shoulder, and chest, not wanting to be selfish.

Chuck rushed over and helped me up, his concern more dramatic than the fall. I assured him I was okay and, in fact, enjoyed the contact. Needless to say, I won that hole and ultimately the round because Chuck was more concerned about me than his golf swing.

All part of the plan.

Whiteboard Goals: Notice

Yeah, stuff happens. Dwelling on the negative, on our hardships, can take over our lives. I don't mean to dismiss the pain and heartaches that we all go through, but we can also look for those moments of joy if we take time to notice. It can be as simple as appreciating that beautiful, magical, late evening light on the eighteenth green as you head for the clubhouse when you're the last group of the day. Or you might notice the innocence and delight of a child at play. Or an older couple walking down the street, holding hands, still looking like they're in love. Your assignment: notice five moments of joy this coming week, or count five blessings you've received. Write them down.

9
LEAD THE WAY

On my last mission trip to Haiti, there was much work to be done, some of it very physically demanding and some not so much. The long-term American missionary in charge of the whole compound would assign the tasks each day. I always loved physical labor, so I was disappointed the first day when my crew was assigned to paint the wall in a computer lab. I desperately wanted to be with the other crew, digging the foundation with shovel and pickaxe out in the sweltering Haitian heat. It had only been two weeks since my ALS diagnosis, and I was denying its effects.

As we did our work in the computer lab, the missionary-in-charge would intermittently burst in to give orders. He would come in chatting in Creole on his cell phone, observe our efforts, bark a quick demand like, "Put those window frames there." And then he would go back to his phone conversation and be gone. I did not see him do an ounce of manual work all week. This was everything I disrespected in a "leader." Now I understand there are cultural differences in that country, but there are better ways to deal with people and to lead. Luckily, throughout my life I have seen many examples of what it means to lead by example.

One of those examples came from Anthony Johnson, AJ as he was called. AJ had played running back in the NFL for eleven years with more than five-thousand rushing and receiving yards. After his career on the field ended, he became the team chaplain for the Jacksonville Jaguars. He had been chaplain for a number of years before my arrival. This man practiced what he preached in every aspect of his life that I could see. We got pretty close in my ten-month stint as a Jag. I expect it was because I desperately needed someone to lead me to the next phase of my spiritual life, and he was open to taking on a willing, moldable man anxious to grow in his faith.

Everyone I met who knew AJ respected him, as I quickly did. AJ was a man of action, and I followed him. I followed him to churches where we spoke. I followed him to soup kitchens to serve the hungry. I followed him to the track to work out and watch his son play football. Heck, I followed him to Costa Rica for a mission trip, twice. He was quick to act and slow to speak. To a guy like me, that was infectious.

In Costa Rica, we served an organization called SCORE International. We had the honor of installing a chain-link fence with barbed wire along the top. This would be the first step in building a mission compound with school buildings, housing for unwed mothers, and a sports field. The entire property was about the size of two football fields, and we were to fence it in three days. We were pumped and up for the job.

We split into two crews, one to dig the postholes and one to mix and handle the cement. AJ and I were going to dig holes. Everybody gave sweat and blood to put that fence up, but the "Diggers for Life," as we named ourselves, took exceptional pride in the difficulty of our task. We all earned our blisters and backaches, but I'll never forget the way AJ led by example. Tough job? He was the first to volunteer. He pushed physically like a twenty-four-year-old football player and led like a wiser older man. All with humility—in other words, he didn't let his ego get in the way of getting the job done.

Now this is the type of person I want to follow. Even more so, this is the type of individual and servant leader that I want to be. Leading by example is powerful and effective.

Lead by Example

As a football player, we always respected a coach who had played the game at a high level. We could respect that he had been where we were and done what he was asking us to do. Even if he couldn't lead by example in the moment, in a way he already had. On the contrary, a coach who had never played was tougher to respect. It often felt as if we were being asked to do impossible things by someone who had never done them himself.

That being said, there are effective ways to lead, even when leading by example isn't an option. I believe that a good leader finds a way to show dedication and contribution to the cause. It may not be in a physical way, but the leader must make clear his care for the cause and his respect for those doing a demanding task. The CEO who worked his way to the top from the mailroom or sales floor has no trouble getting respect from employees, even though he probably doesn't break his back to make sales anymore. But the CEO given the position because of birthright will have much more trouble getting the same respect. They both hold the same position, but one has a stronger platform to lead from. Position does not dictate leadership. We follow people we respect and who take action. People follow people who live out what they talk about.

Like the legendary William Wallace tells Robert the Bruce in the movie Braveheart, "Your title gives you claim to the throne of our country, but people don't follow title, they follow courage." I've seen plenty of people in leadership positions who were not being followed. It's not the position, it's the person.

I found myself in a leadership role at a young age. Maybe it was because I was bigger and taller than most kids. Maybe it was my personality. Maybe it was my bowl haircut. Whatever the case, my classmates followed my lead. (Getting my classmates to cough every time the teacher said a certain word wasn't my finest hour.) At first, I saw this role as a burden, as it being restrictive. I had to set a good example. I had to do things right. I had to be more careful and aware of my attitudes and morals. Worst of all, I was held to a higher standard. Man, I hated that. As a youngster, this was rough because I just wanted to do my thing without the added pressure. I didn't want to set the standard or lead the pack. It wasn't fair or fun that they expected more from me. That's how I felt until high school, when I realized that it's always better to embrace who you are rather than fight your God-given characteristics.

Somewhere around the end of ninth grade, it started to sink in. I don't know whether it was my coaches, teachers, or parents (probably all three), but I started to see benefits to being a leader. As I excelled in the athletic arena, my teammates followed me even more. When I demanded more, they gave more. When I approved or disapproved of something, they took my stance. When tough things happened, they looked for my response. The harder I worked, the harder the team worked. And we got better. Coaches would lean on me because I could sway the team. Suddenly the responsibility could be used for good. I could see the benefit of a higher standard.

I began to enjoy and appreciate the ability to help others improve. And by helping them improve, it improved our team. Win-win.

I didn't embrace leadership off the field as quickly, probably because I couldn't see as much benefit. I didn't want to lead all the time, only when it was convenient for me. I wasn't interested in making friends and influencing people off the field. I didn't want to win homecoming king (and I didn't); I just wanted to have fun. But ultimately it was sports that prompted good behavior and leadership off the field, too, because apparently carrying yourself as a leader isn't a sometimes thing. It's not that you have to lead in every facet of your life, but your character does have to be consistent. If not, a character flaw displayed in one context may lose you the respect of your peers in another, which undermines your leadership.

Leadership has really been a big part of my story. I hated winning the "leadership awards" in life because I wanted to win the MVP, but it was a big part of who I was, and deep down I knew that I was respected by the right people for my athletic ability and leadership.

The height of my athletic leadership came in my fifth NFL season when my Titans teammates voted me as their special teams captain. I had been there one year and obviously made an impression. The two years I spent as the Titans Special Teams Captain is my proudest feat as a football player. The reason it meant so much to me was because it indicated my level of play was high, and that I was trusted, respected, and followed by my teammates. It was a great honor for me.

So what changed from my first three teams to my fourth? Did I figure something out? Become a better player? Learn how to lead? Did it all just come together for me? I argue no. Sure, I kept improving as I learned the tricks of the trade and my knowledge of the game grew, but I had been productive and reliable for every team. For one reason or another, it just didn't work out for me to stick around. The lesson is this: if you know you're on the right track, keep going. Even if the results aren't what you want yet, stick to your guns. Don't let outside forces or lack of results keep you from your goals. If you believe that you're doing all you can to make it happen, then stay the course. That's all I did. I was ever evaluating what I was doing to make sure there wasn't a better way; I believed I was doing the right things. So I just had to keep being me, working and believing that it would all pay off. More often than not, a little "sticktoitiveness," persistence, is the final ingredient in a victory sandwich. Ultimately, I found a team that valued me enough to keep me around for a while. So be you, and it will all work out.

Learn Leadership

Can someone adopt or achieve the necessary traits to lead? I believe they can. Legendary football coach Vince Lombardi said, "Leaders aren't born, they are made. And they are made just like anything else, through hard work. And that's the price we'll have to pay to achieve that goal, or any goal." A man can learn to lead just as he can learn to be honest. It may not be easy, but it is definitely learnable. One can learn to look out for others and teach them. One can see someone leading and copy his or her ways. Someone can learn how to gain the attention of others and influence their thinking or behavior. It would be hard to deny that those traits can be learned, but it might be easier to deny it than to actually learn them and take on the additional responsibilities.

On top of that, I believe that everyone should lead at one time or another in some capacity. I can't believe that some people are just meant to follow others their whole lives. There are many different ways to lead, and many different capacities. I have to believe that we all are given a passion to discover and pursue and that in that pursuit we can lead others.

But lots of people avoid leadership by saying they aren't a leader, "It's not who I am." It's much easier to not be a leader than to assume the risk and responsibility required of a leader. But you would be selling yourself short. Copping out, actually. Taking the easy road. Being average. I don't believe that would be your best self.

There is a leader in you.

You may not be a natural-born leader or be the best speaker or be comfortable giving instructions, but those are just excuses. You can lead even without those traits. You must first embrace the idea and start to see yourself as such, but you can lead. Once you are willing, the rest can happen. Embrace the leader inside, step outside of your comfort zone, and people will follow.

There are all types of leaders in the world. Which type are you? There are silent but strong leaders. They don't say much, but their actions speak volumes. There are boisterous and enthusiastic leaders. They can stir up a crowd quickly, and the bigger the crowd the better. Some leaders humbly go about their duties while others require much fanfare. Some leaders are experts in their fields while others are the hardest working. It takes all kinds of people to embrace and respond to all kinds of different leadership styles.

The greatest impact comes when you lead right where you are. Sure, some people are thrust into the limelight to lead larger audiences, but it all starts right where we are. We must lead at home, at our jobs, and in our communities. Leadership is non-stop, and while a good leader knows when to be quiet or even subdued, ultimately he or she knows that someone is always watching. Therefore, who you are must be consistent. You don't need to be given a position of power or authority to lead. Sometimes it takes someone from a lower rank to step up and lead. Maybe all of your fellow colleagues are divided and disgruntled. Well, you don't need to be donned a leader to use your influence to calm the ranks and bridge the gap. That's leadership.

These are plenty of ways to lead effectively, and a good leader knows when and how to lead in different ways. But like always, it's best to be yourself. Don't force yourself to be someone else. There may be a time when a leader needs to motivate their followers. Some would say this calls for a big, pump-up pep talk, like we see in all great sports movies. Some leaders shine in this situation and can stand up and deliver powerful words that motivate the troops to action. But maybe this isn't you. If not, don't force it. It will come out awkward and you won't get the results you're after. Instead, find an alternative form of motivation that suits you. Maybe you're better off having one-on-one conversations with your teammates, or maybe you can offer them some sort of reward. Maybe you can find a way to shake things from the norm and invigorate those around you. Figure out a way to lead using your skillset. You will be much more effective this way. To be the most effective leader you can be, you must be yourself.

I'm reminded of the story my pastor, Pete Wilson, told me about the early years of Cross Point, the church he and his wife started in Nashville in 2002. He was twenty-seven at the time. When you start a new church, Pete said people are attracted to something new because many didn't like what they had before, and they come with an agenda.

"I would tell people what they wanted to hear," Pete said. "They might say, 'We want this kind of women's ministry,' or 'this kind of music.' And it's easy when you're desperate for warm bodies to say, 'Yeah, one day we could totally see a women's ministry like this.' But in the back of your mind you're not seeing it. It's flat-out lying, but in that moment it's really easy to convince yourself."

Pete said there's a cost to that because people eventually want to cash in on all the promises made. "A good two years into the church, it almost imploded." It wasn't until Pete had the courage to stand behind the vision that he felt God had given him that the church really started to be effective and grow. He had to be true to himself.

"The thing I've learned is that it's hard to be a dream chaser and a people pleaser all at the same time," he said. "Everyone loves you until you lead. And so when you lead—and leadership requires tough decisions—everybody is not always happy, and not everyone is going to see the vision that you feel like you have."

Today Cross Point Church has six campuses in the greater Nashville area, serving eight-thousand people a week. Not only has the church grown, so has Cross Point's vision. Recently, this community has been dreaming of planting fifteen churches in the next five years. "To say that out loud scared me to death, but it energized everyone around here," Pete said. "I've learned making your goals and dreams public invites others to participate with you."

The growth of Cross Point wouldn't surprise Marcus Cobb. You remember Marcus, my rap buddy and founder of Jammber, the company that works to get musicians paid faster—and, oh yeah, the guy whose goal is to be the first black tech billionaire. He said, "I've seen it in churches. I've seen it in music. I've seen it in business, in nonprofits. Good leadership begets growth."

Marcus went on to say that he hasn't met anyone who cannot learn to be a leader. "I think we're all leaders in some capacity every day. And I don't know any leaders who are not constant students of leadership." He said all the leaders he knows are constantly reading, constantly self-evolving, constantly getting feedback from peers and mentors.

And, Marcus said, the good leaders want to create success for those he or she leads. "The only way to do that is to be a servant leader. For me, that means not thinking of yourself any more highly than others. You do it because you want the job done well, you want your team treated well. You're leading people where they want to go together."

Leading the Whole Person

Marcus, when he was getting Jammber established in Nashville, turned to the Entrepreneur Center for guidance and expertise. The center is now led by Mike Brody-Waite. But before going to the Entrepreneur Center, Mike was the CEO and cofounder of InQuicker, a company that provided software to hospitals that allowed patients to go online and schedule appointments for multiple levels of care, dramatically increasing access to healthcare. Under his leadership, InQuicker grew at an astounding rate. InQuicker was named one of *Inc.* magazine's Inc. 500, and his company was named one of the "Best Places to Work in Nashville" four out of five years. Mike was named "Healthcare Entrepreneur of the Year" by the Chamber of Commerce and "Most Admired CEO" by the Nashville Business Journal.

Whether your passion is building a creative career, a non-profit organization, or a business, you'll find Mike's leadership philosophy and approach to life instructive, even inspirational.

Mike will tell you he's a recovering addict and alcoholic. "I'm in a twelve-step program. I've been in it since 2002, which is one of the reasons why my values are what they are," he said. One of those values is love. "During my first ninety days in recovery, someone gave me a definition of love, a simple definition: 'Love is when I want what is best for you, whether it includes me or not.'"

Those are words worth remembering—in business, marriage, relationships, friendship. Love is when you want the best for that person. And you want the best for him or her, even if that doesn't include you, even if that doesn't benefit you personally.

Mike said he wasn't always the benefactor of that type of unconditional love growing up, but he found it in his twelve-step program. "I entered a community that says, 'We're going to love you until you can love yourself. And we're going to help you save your life, and it's all for free, and it's all just because someone did it for us.'"

Mike told of the time he was ten months clean and moving to a new home. "The odds are I'm going to relapse at any time," he said. "But my sponsor throws me his keys to his $50,000 Avalanche and says, 'Bring it back when you're done.' That kind of trust and love, it's rare." In this community, Mike said he started figuring out his leadership style. He wasn't going to wear the typical entrepreneur or CEO mask. He was going to focus on embracing vulnerability and authenticity and a foundation of absolute unconditional love.

"In a business context, what that means is an employee is a person. It's not just their professional life I should care about. It's their personal life," he said. Granted, Mike knows that there is a lot of talk about work-life balance, including at Dell where he worked before cofounding InQuicker. "I had a boss that said, 'I care about work-life balance. I want you to take care of your families.' And then when people would send him a work e-mail at 2 a.m., it's like, 'Look at Danny.

He's working so hard.' And when people went on vacation with their families, he would talk [crap] about them. I set out to create a company that really followed through on loving the employees, even if that meant that I as an owner would profit less."

Mike said that if an employee told him, for example, he couldn't come to a customer meeting because he had a child that was sick, his first reaction would be self-centered fear—"Oh, what's going to happen to our success?" Then the higher self that he learned from his twelve-step experience would kick in. "I want what's best for that person whether it includes me or not. And what's best for that person is for him to know that not only is it best, not only is it okay for that person to take care of his child, but I wouldn't dare want him to be here."

As another example of loving the whole person, Mike said he had all these people working so hard for the company and a lot of them had families, so after a day of business work, they had to work at home. He thought if he could carve out three or four hours of their work day, then they could actually take time for themselves. With that in mind, he told people to leave at noon on Friday.

"But they wouldn't leave," Mike said. "To try to make people understand that I wasn't doing the thing that my boss at Dell did, I sent an e-mail calendar invite for 1:00 p.m. on Friday that said, 'Leave the office or die.'" He said he believes that if you really honor who an employee is as a whole person, that person will love the company and everyone else wholly. "With the company leaders practicing unconditional love, what we called employee love, we started seeing everyone in the company doing it for each other."

Mike says as the company grew, he and his cofounder, Kurt Essenmacher—who, he calls a man of faith, a family man—were both seeing people genuinely showing love to each other through their actions at the office, because they set this tone of unconditional love.

"So I'm sitting in this meeting with Holly, my director of finance, and she said so-and-so bought another person this special tea that they liked because they had a cold or something, and they put it on the company card. And one of the account executives didn't have a babysitter, so Kurt is doing an expense report to pay for the sitter. And so-and-so had a customer, and they had a bad day, so she sent her a massage certificate. 'We've got to reign this in!' she said. I replied, 'Holly, we've got to lean into this.'"

Mike went on to say as a way of leaning in, they created a fund that employees could use to support this gifting behavior through a make-my-day type of account. Every quarter, every employee received fifty dollars to make each other's day. "It's the tangible mechanism that reinforces our value, which was to do what was best for employees," he said.

Lead for Growth

Early in the company's history, Mike and Kurt sat down and said they were going to challenge everything that sucked about having bosses. They decided that they wanted to focus on individuals, recognizing the complexities of their lives. And they didn't want to just give it lip service, but they wanted to prove through their actions that they meant it. It wasn't about "building a team" but about "building a person." "They translated their philosophy to these three beliefs:

1. An Employee Is a Person. Each employee is a beautiful person with a life that is so much bigger than what they do for work. Yet they spend as much or more time working. It is potentially the community in which they spend the most time!

2. Love and Nurture the "Whole Person." Each person is not just an "account manager" but also a "mother" or "sister" or "friend" or leader in their community, etc. Each person has their own strengths, weaknesses, fears, and dreams that they take with them no matter where they work or who they work with. Our leaders must love, nurture, and inspire each person without discriminating between what is "work" and what is "personal." A whole employee is a whole person. We love and nurture them wholly.

3. The Whole Person Will Love and Nurture the Whole Company. There is a saying that "it takes a village to raise a child." In our case, each person is a member of the "village" and the "child" is the company. Here's where it gets exponentially awesome: if we love and nurture each whole person, he or she will love and nurture both the company and each other in ways we couldn't imagine.

Mike, in summarizing these beliefs, said, "It's really as simple as this: love and nurture the 'whole person' instead of just the employee. If we do, we will have a strong, fully equipped and effective staff. More importantly we will see ourselves and others grow as people, not just employees. After all, isn't that kind of the point? I mean, who in this life is just an employee? Not me. It's time to stop building teams and starting building people. Loving the whole person includes considering each person's unique perception and situation, helping each person achieve something they didn't think was possible, and know and support what matters most outside of work.

These beliefs stem from the leadership values and characteristics they identified as follows:

- **Faith:** Lead from a place of humble confidence. No place for ego here.

- **Integrity:** Do the next right thing no matter what. No matter the cost.

- **Transparency:** Have the trust and courage to seek and lean into the uncomfortable truth.

- **Grow:** Have the courage to ask for help and share with the team our growing edges.

- **Team:** Help people know which part of the body they are and why that is so valuable.

- **Love:** Embrace every opportunity to love and nurture the whole person.

I've given you all these examples, not only to encourage you to be a leader—to evolve and learn about leadership—but also to think creatively about what your leadership and values could look like wherever you find yourself, whether as a musician working with other musicians, as an artist working with your social media team, as a sales rep in a big department, as someone launching your dream company, or as a mom or dad, a teammate or employee.

Whiteboard Goals: Get Your Leadership On

What would you adapt from the above examples of leadership values and characteristics, or what would you add to create an ethical, compassionate environment to impact your world? How could you express your values in a tangible way? What aspects of your best boss, your favorite coach, your most admired leaders would you want to incorporate into your own leadership philosophy? And most important, write down areas where you could take a leadership role. Take a few minutes—or more than a few minutes—and dream of what you could do as a leader, what guidelines you would develop. Then write them down.

SHARE THE
ROAD

10
MENTOR AND BE MENTORED

One of the best examples of leadership I've found is coach-turned-broadcaster Tony Dungy. I never had the privilege of playing for him, but I have studied him from a distance and read his books. I have always admired the way Tony led with character in a world where integrity often takes a backseat to money and winning.

He often went against the grain in order to stick to his values. When most organizations worked their coaches all hours of the night, Coach Dungy displayed his value for family by sending coaches home at a reasonable time. Despite his unorthodox methods, his teams enjoyed much success.

Possibly my biggest takeaway from Tony Dungy is his philosophy of what he calls "Mentor Leadership." This is the idea that the good leaders are mentoring others as they lead. It's the idea of pouring into others, even to the point where they may be benefitting far more than you. Tony was notorious for losing assistant coaches. He was mentoring them so well they were getting bigger jobs elsewhere. Tony believed that he should lead so well and so selflessly that he was preparing people to take his job. And ultimately, he did just that. Tony believed that he was in his position to serve others and that his personal needs would be met through that service, even to the point of losing his job. So as he was constantly losing his best assistant coaches, therefore making it tougher on himself and his team, he continued to win. I'm inspired by the thought of the impact Coach Dungy is still having as those men continue to spread what they have learned.

On the player side, I think the best mentor-leader I've ever had the privilege of knowing was Matt Hasselbeck. Matt came to Nashville during my second year at the Titans. We had just drafted quarterback Jake Locker with our first round pick. When you draft a guy eighth overall, he's going to play. You've already declared he's your guy. And it was Matt's job, in his fourteenth NFL season, to mentor this young superstar. It takes a special kind of person to take on that role, knowing you're not the guy. Keep in mind that Matt had all the skills, abilities, and proven track record to be the starting quarterback. He was a three-time Pro Bowler, and had led the Seattle Seahawks to six playoff appearances and a Super Bowl appearance.

So from the jump, I respected his resume. From what I saw, Matt was the ultimate mentor-leader. The quarterback is always looked at to be a leader—the problem is they don't always fulfill that role—but Matt did. He had a way to engage everyone on the team—not just the receivers, or the backs, or the offense, but everyone. Matt would ask them questions about their lives, about their families, about their girlfriends. He would really pour himself into them. Because of that, I wanted to be around him. After practice, I might ask him what he was up to. Sometimes he would say he was off to his daughter's basketball practice. My response: "Cool. I'm going with you."

I think the number-one thing about being a mentor-leader is attitude and humility. If your attitude is that you're the best and you deserve more—a very "me-me-me" attitude—you're not going to be a good mentor. But someone with a humble attitude says, "The good I will do as a mentor is more important than the good that I will get from pursuing selfish gains." That was Matt's attitude. He knew that if the coaches played him, they would have a better chance of winning than with the inexperienced rookie. But the coaches asked him to develop Jake, so that is what he did to the best of his ability. That's the ultimate example of a team player.

As it turns out, Jake was often hurt during the seasons and, at the drop of a hat, Matt would step in, and make plays and lead, winning several games. The guy had street cred, which made him even more respected as a mentor-leader. Through observing Matt, the best advice I learned was not to let other people dictate what you think about yourself or what you do.

Mentor Vision

Thinking of Matt, and looking back at my life, I can't help but be thankful for the people who have given so much to me. There are countless people who have shared with me their time, wisdom, experience, knowledge, and even money—all with the goal of enriching my life. It would have been impossible to reach the heights that I have without this generosity.

I'll never forget Mr. Bargerstock: the sixth grade geography teacher who happened to have played fullback at Ohio State and had a body fit for a WWF wrestler. He was known for snatching kids by their shirts and carrying them one-handed out of class. He convinced my dad (without physical force, I hope!) that I needed to play for his middle school football team rather than the city team I was currently on. He saw something special in me and wanted to coach me. I was only in eighth grade, but he took me to the weight room and taught me how to lift. "Nobody else will teach you right," he said, "and it's time." I'll never forget that and I'm forever grateful. I am convinced that his belief in my future went even further than the training itself. He didn't have to do that. There wasn't anything in it for him. But he did. My first mentor.

Coach Hudkins took over my high school football team after my freshman season. Not only did he start our school's first junior varsity team and a strength and conditioning program, he changed my whole perspective on the game. I admired his knowledge of the game, the way he communicated, and most of all, his passion and love for what we were doing. He blew the roof off of my game and made me believe I could do anything if I was willing to work for it. I flourished in his off-season program and thrived in his football system. I got exponentially stronger and faster. I fed off his energy and strove to multiply his fire. Our individual successes complemented each other, but I know he went out of his way for me on countless occasions. He walked me through the recruiting process and helped me choose a university to attend. His approval meant a lot to me, so we made the final decision in his kitchen, calling Coach Perles of Michigan State to decline their scholarship offer and Coach Vanderlinden of Penn State to accept theirs. He remained a mentor for many years, someone I would call for advice in tough spots, like when Penn State moved me from running back to linebacker (tragic at the time), and when I was cut the first time from an NFL team. His message was ever steady: "Control what you can. Outwork and outsmart them."

Many of my mentors were spiritual mentors. These men, through various stages of my life, cared more about my personal growth than my football career. They not only gave me their time, but they cared for me. We would discuss tough topics like marriage and sexuality. We would study various books of the Bible or other faith-based books. In doing these things, they helped me navigate life.

For example, I started meeting with Mark Kieft, the pastor of my church when I was in high school. A group of us would meet at Burger King on Saturday mornings to study the Bible. He even showed us the strength of the Lord (or just teamwork) one morning. As we arrived, a woman going through the drive-through opened her door and reached down to retrieve some dropped cash. In the process, she wedged herself in the door, stuck between her truck and the building. All the while, the truck was in drive, so it was slowly edging along the building, sure to crush her. With minimal drama, and not even a pause for prayer, Mark climbed in the bed of the truck, and reached in and turned it off. A few of us lifted the front end of the truck, freeing the woman. Burger King didn't even pay for our meal! Mark demonstrated what a Good Samaritan looks like.

Tim McGill, another mentor, was the leader of Athletes in Action at Penn State. I must have met with him one-on-one just about every week for my five years on campus. Tim showed me how to be a committed, faithful man of God, always willing to serve.

Once I got to the NFL, I made sure to connect with the team chaplains. A team chaplain isn't paid by the team, but hangs around the team, holds Bible studies, and makes himself available to anybody in need of counsel, often helping players deal with life in the NFL. I remember gathering myself (keeping myself from crying uncontrollably) in Mike Bunkley's office on my way out of the building after being cut by the Panthers. Anthony Johnson, as I've mentioned, led me on multiple service projects around Jacksonville and took me on my first mission trip. Reggie Pleasant mentored me for years in Tennessee and stood by me through my diagnosis. These men poured into me knowledge, wisdom, and love. They helped me navigate through the difficult and unpredictable life as an NFL player.

Find or Be Found

One thing about mentors though, sometimes they show up and assume the role, and sometimes you have to seek them out and ask to be mentored. Sometimes you choose a seat, and you just happen to sit next to Na'il Diggs. I was a rookie and he was a seven-year vet. He looked over at me in our first meeting and said, "Get out your pen and paper and write everything down." And I did, and he mentored me for the entire year I sat next to him.

Sometimes you knock on their door and ask them to spend intentional time with you each week, like I did with AJ and Reggie. Yet oftentimes it's much less formal and you simply tag along with someone you want to learn from. People are surprisingly willing to share what they know even in competitive situations—especially when someone asks humbly. In my experience, people want to help others but don't often seek out ways to do so. Consequently, when an opportunity to mentor shows up at the door, they gladly oblige. I've done this over and over throughout my life. There have been a couple guys along the way who selfishly didn't have time or didn't want to bother, but the willing far outweigh the unwilling.

There isn't always a clear line between mentor and friend, and there doesn't have to be. We typically think of mentors as being older, but that doesn't have to be the case either. To me, it reflects back on the principle of surrounding yourself with good people. People you want to be like; people you can learn from and who will positively influence you.

Maybe they are mentors but maybe they are just good dudes. Hopefully, you can teach and influence each other.

Commandments of Mentorship

Being a mentor is a beautiful thing, as it is far better to give than to receive. As the flow of life goes, to whom much is given, he or she has much to give. Whatever the philosophical saying, I feel greatly responsible to give, give, give. I mean, I have been given so much! So many people have spent time pouring their wisdom into me. What a shame to keep that to myself. I must pass it on. What do you have that needs to be shared? Who needs to hear or see it? Don't keep it in. There's no better way to honor your mentor than to mentor another. Who has mentored you? Given invaluable advice or experience? Kept you from seemingly inevitable pitfalls? Put their arm around your shoulder and guided you in the right direction?

Maybe you're wondering just how to get started as a mentor. What exactly should you do? Of course, there are a thousand ways to be a mentor, but if you're looking for some guidelines, consider those that mentors at the Entrepreneur Center use. Adapt them for your own mentoring situations:

> **1. Listen actively.** Listening is the first principle of effective mentoring. Without it nothing else works. Listening actively means paying attention not only to the words, but also for tone and body language. Make notes of

what you are hearing, your observations, and questions you will ask later to clarify what you heard. This also helps you to focus on listening and not talking.

2. Question powerfully. Knowing what questions to ask comes from filtering what you have heard through your experience. Questioning powerfully draws the mentee's attention to the challenges to making his or her idea successful.

3. Communicate directly. Make your feedback clear and direct. The golden rule of mentoring is to honor the mentees courage for putting their ideas out there to be judged, but never give the idea a free ride. The worst thing a mentor can do is allow mentees to believe their ideas are better than they really are.

4. Inspire independence. Mentees have to do their own work. There is no free ride. Mentors are to guide mentees to think about things from a different perspective. You can help them avoid dead ends and wasted effort, but pursuing one's passion is a marathon—let them discover that they have the endurance for it.

5. Build rapport. Set expectations of the relationship early. Your job is to listen, share your experience, and treat them with respect.

Their job is to accept the feedback and do something with it.

6. Assign homework. Help mentees address an immediate challenge or key assumption that needs testing by having them take some sort of action. Be specific, allowing mentees to clarify issues on their own without your telling them what needs to be done. Make it simple and executable. They learn more from what they discover on their own than what you tell them.

7. Be an unbiased observer. Don't tell them, "Do this, this, and this." Ask first what they are thinking about any given problem. You can give an example of what an answer might look like, but avoid advising them on what they should do.

8. Hold them accountable. A mentor is a wise friend and counselor, but you must hold them accountable to execute homework and exhibit improvement. They may do things differently than you would, but they need to explore the territory you opened up for them.

9. Always mentor and be mentored. You can always be mentoring. Whether it be for two minutes in the hall or an hour at lunchtime. It's also important to be open—a mentee may impart insights and wisdom to you as well. The best mentors are the ones who can admit they don't have all (or even most) of the answers. You don't have to know it all.

10. Know when it's time to move on. Mentoring someone, like everything else in life, has a season. At some point, it will come time for you to step back from your active mentor role. You will know when the time is right, a time when you can be a supporter and friend.

Write to Impress

When you write something down, it's a commitment or declaration; it says, "I'm really serious about this." Writing things down, as you'll see from the following story, led Britnie Turner Keane to one of her most influential mentors. Britnie, as you recall, went from a twenty-one-year old rookie waitress real estate investor wannabe who was living out of her car to the largest infill housing developer in Nashville in less than five years.

Always reading about real estate, always seeking advice about growing her business, Britnie was one of thirty high-level entrepreneurs invited to Richard Branson's private island, Necker Island in the British Virgin Islands. Branson, as you probably know, is founder and chairman of Virgin Group, which includes more than two-hundred companies, one of which is Virgin Galactic, a space-tourism company! (How cool is that?)

As he was speaking, Britnie said she was feverishly writing down everything he said. "And afterward, he cames up to me and said I was the one he wanted to mentor."

She was surprised and, of course, pumped. She asked him why her. Richard said, "Of the thirty people—who all were super-excited to see me when they arrived—you were the only one taking notes. This shows me you care, you are here to learn, and you will actually execute on what I am teaching you."

All her mentor relationships, Britnie said, developed because of her note taking, because it signaled she felt that what they were saying was important enough to write down. And it's advice she passes on to others looking for mentors. "Also," Britnie said, "a mentor should be someone you want to be like. The world will always have lots of opinions on what you should be doing, but only listen to people you want to be like."

She likewise passes on her knowledge through speaking engagements at colleges (where we first met), and other organizations, including a speech to the United Nations as part of the Global Diversity Leadership Exchange. Britnie mentors students through her company's internship program and mentors her staff as well. "People don't just work here. We teach them how to buy homes, about equity, credit, taxes, investment savings, and long-term financial strategy. We set them up to succeed in life."

Whiteboard Goals: Choose Your Mentor

Do you have mentors in your life? If not, you need to find them. Who is it that you admire? Intentionally spend more time with them. Who has accomplished something that you desire to do or is doing it now? Who excels in an area in which you seek to improve? Watch them closely. If you don't currently have a mentor, write down two or three names. Then pick one and send an e-mail asking him or her if you could meet for a short time—in their office or over coffee near their workplace—to help you gain some insight into their area of expertise. If the first person declines, go to the next name. When you meet, take notes. At the end of your meeting, ask if you can contact them from time to time with other questions. As the relationship grows and your mentor-in-progress sees you're serious about learning more from them, you can suggest regular meetings. And you're on your way to a solid mentor relationship.

11

Good
Investments

When I got drafted, I instantly became a millionaire—at least that's what everyone thought. The general perception of an NFL player is that he makes millions of dollars, but that's because all the public hears about are the big multimillion-dollar contracts. ESPN didn't report about my rookie league minimum $280,000 salary. Truth is, I made less than a million in my first three seasons combined, and that's before Uncle Sam took his half. Don't get me wrong, I know that's good money. Very good. But it's far from millionaire status, and given the less than four-year career average, most guys never get there.

Regardless of whether you have made millions or if you barely get by, we are all called to do the best with what we've been given. The same principles that apply to money apply to our gifts and abilities. To pursue your passion and make an impact, you have to use what you have for things that matter.

Good Investments

No doubt, we live in a culture that tells us we need more stuff, and the more we have, the happier we will be. If you live in a mansion, have a home on the beach, rare cars, fancy clothes, and cash piled up, but die without true friends and meaningful relationships, without making an impact, without making the world a better place, then you didn't live a rich life where it mattered. Cars are fun. Jewelry is nice. Houses are great. I have all of that (okay, minus the jewelry), but I promise you, they don't guarantee happiness. In fact, in 2010 Princeton did a huge study—involving 450,000 people—raising the question of whether or not money buys happiness. The study measured emotional well-being, that is, how individuals reported their everyday experience with such emotions as joy, anxiety, sadness, anger, and affection. As income went up, so did emotional well-being—but only to a point. Beyond $75,000, emotional well-being did not go up.[1]

Great, you say, I'll take that seventy-five grand and be happy. (Yes, only about one in three make that much, according to the US Census Bureau.[2]) And true, money is not easy to come by. Most of us work very hard to earn it; it represents our time and effort. So why aren't we more careful and purposeful with our money? Why are we so flippant in our spending habits? Our culture of instant gratification dictates our tendency to buy what we want, right now. The question becomes "Why can't I have it now?" This leads to purchases we can't afford, which holds us hostage to the money we owe. On the other hand, waiting to purchase an item until we can afford it brings with it the personal satisfaction of knowing that we earned it, it's ours, and we don't owe anyone for it. Being in control of how your money is spent is worth the struggle. It may seem like an uphill battle with no end in sight, but the outcome is worth it. Don't give up on being disciplined with your finances. Being weighed down by credit cards and debt makes life feel like prison and every decision seem burdensome. There are a lot of helpful books on how to manage your finances—check them out for some in-depth help.

In the meantime, follow a simple rule: spend slower than you earn. I knew that I wouldn't be a professional athlete forever and the big paychecks would stop coming in, so keeping up with the Joneses wasn't smart. I wanted my lifestyle to catch up to my bank account rather than my bank account having to catch up with my lifestyle. I didn't need to show the world my value by what I wore or drove. I saw everyday money decisions as my key to making the hard-earned football money last and last. I was okay with flying coach, eating at inexpensive restaurants, and driving the same truck I'd had for years. These decisions compounded daily in my favor, but they could have easily compounded negatively had my decision been to constantly spend more.

I saw it over and over again, my teammates spending like there was no tomorrow. The newest gadgets, the hottest cars, trips to donate their cash to the casino owners of Las Vegas (is that donation tax deductible?). I could write a whole book on the spending habits of pro athletes. It would be fascinating and quite entertaining, but I'll spare us the embarrassment.

Yes, even I once spent $3,000 on dinner. Lucky for me, I learned quickly from mistakes of those around me and heeded the advice of loved ones warning me to be wise. More than anything, though, I was scared. That's right, scared I wouldn't make the team, or last long in the league, leaving the game broke. Maybe it wasn't fear so much as a healthy, realistic view of my situation. As confident as I was in myself, I still knew the possibility of outside forces derailing my dream. So I was conservative with money. I realize this is not the typical situation, and most people would love to have the problem of having more than they know what to do with. But the point is this: it's not how much you make that counts, but how much you keep. It's crazy, but I know people who make $50,000 or less who have kept more of their salary than guys who made a million dollars in a year! Wild but true. This is as applicable to you as it is to me. To be our best, we must make the most with what we have.

Here's another funny truth when it comes to money: the more you have, the harder it is to give away. It doesn't make great sense, but it's true. As the bank account grows, so does the need to keep it there. More and more people want your money, so the pressure of what to do with it mounts. You now have almost unlimited choices of charitable investments as well. If you do want to give some away, how do you choose between the thousands of charity options? It's easier to just put your money with an advisor and live comfortably, being prepared for any potential danger in the future. Problem is, that's not making the best use of what you have. Sure, save for the future. And definitely take care of your family. But find ways to impact the world for the better. Maybe you can support a local charity. Maybe you send a team to do disaster relief. Maybe you find someone who is down and out and provide that boost they need to get back on track. There are a countless ways to do it, but you must do something. Start right where you are, big or small, then as your income grows your generosity can grow also. Giving is essential to living an impactful life. As you can tell, one of my favorite ways to give is through international missions trips, which have been a big part of my adult life.

Back to the Amazon

It was my second trip to the Amazon but my first with Josiah. I was so impressed by this nineteen-year-old missionary kid. He was fluent in Portuguese and English and was a hard worker. I was most impressed by his spirit. He just wanted to serve. He told me about his dream to become a pilot and fly supplies into the jungle and reach people in need of emergency medical help in the Amazon. Neither he nor his family had much money, so they couldn't afford college. I left that trip knowing that I wanted to help this young guy. I knew that whatever he pursued, he would shine. He just needed a boost. What could I do for him? Give him some money? Send him to school? After some prayer, I decided to help him pursue his passion to learn how to fly.

Josiah and his brother had someone agree to teach them. They, however, would have to pay for plane usage and flight time, so I helped to fund them with what they needed to get through flight school. Once they learned how to fly, I would continue to support their efforts to help people in Brazil. A life of impact requires some leaps of faith and stretches of generosity. Who knows the effect that support will have on Josiah and the countless people his mission will reach. Now *that* is money well spent.

Some people might say, I don't have money to do things like that. Well, those people might be missing the point. I watched my parents in amazement as I grew up. On a teacher's salary with mom staying home to take care of four huge boys, I watched my parents give and give. I knew that every month they gave a check to church. Who knows how much, but they gave consistently. They gave what they had. I didn't understand it, but they seemed to be always loaning someone a car or letting someone live with us for a time. They saw needs and used what they had to meet those needs. A woman from our church lived with us for a few months while figuring out a tough personal situation. A high school senior stayed with us for her last semester, when her home situation wasn't healthy. My parents lived a life of giving. All the meals they have served guests and monetary sacrifices they have made, I guarantee they consider that money well spent.

Give Money, Keep Friends

Pursuing your dreams and your passions takes not only hard work, but fellow travelers. In addition to mentors and like-minded coworkers, we all need the support provided through close relationships and true friends.

I am privileged to have that kind of special bond with my three biological brothers. But beyond that, I have been lucky enough over the years to have friends that are as close to me as brothers. I remember track season my senior year of high school. I had lost only one race all year, and I had won the state championship in the 100-meter dash the previous year—so this day at regionals I was favored to win. I had already qualified for the state meet in the long jump earlier in the day and was cruising through the prelims, about 20 yards ahead of my heat, when I slowed to an easier pace and felt a pop. I felt my hamstring give. For a competitor with something to prove, this was devastating, but I was on my way to Penn State to play football, so I knew there were bigger things ahead.

The tough part was calling my brother to tell him I wouldn't be winning that day. Drew was on his way to the meet to catch the finals and do his usual screaming from the finish line. I called him after I tested out the hammy to see if I could still run or not. "Turn around bro, I can't run," I told him.

"What do you mean?" He couldn't fathom what I was saying.

"I tried, I just can't run, bro."

"Can't you wrap it up or something?"

He was baffled that his superstar big brother who never missed a down, a practice, an anything, could be hurt.

It's amazing that this conversation was tougher for me than losing the opportunity to compete in the state track meet, but that's the love and support of a brother. That call wasn't nearly as tough, though, as the ones I would have to make twelve years later. This time, not with news of some minor sports injury, but with a devastating diagnosis. When the letters "ALS" were pinned to my name, I wanted to keep it to myself, protect everybody else, and carry on my way. The thought of dragging those I love through a horrific health journey was maybe even worse than going through it myself.

Breaking the news was the hardest. I did it slowly, texting Drew because I knew I couldn't speak. As difficult as it was, I called my parents who, luckily for me, were with my brother Steve and his wife, which saved me an additional difficult call. Then I called my brother Pete and his wife. What blew me away was not just the response my news evoked from my brothers but from my closest friends.

Of course, I understood the shock and pain from my biological brothers, but I really knew how much I was loved when I shared my news with the friends who had become like brothers to me. I was able to tell Jeff, one of my longest-standing friends, in person. He took the news hard. The bond we have cannot be explained.

Nick, Kevin, and Asa all live across the country, so a phone call would have to do. The depth of our friendships is amazing considering the short time we have known each other. Mandee, my other oldest friend, required a phone call as well. The calls didn't get any easier as I made them. What blew me away, and proved brotherhood to me, was all of their abilities and willingness to show me how much I meant to them by letting their feelings and emotions out. Now, we are talking about men here, tough men. But we are also talking about a death sentence for me from the doctor; therefore, toughness and stereotypical manhood go out the window. I'd usually start with something like, "Hey, you know I've been trying to figure out what's been going on with my body for a while now? Well, I just saw the doctor..." The tone would turn serious, acknowledged by the silence, and there would be no room for anything but the difficult truth. I will cherish those conversations. They were raw and rich. We cried. We hurt. We were real. We yelled at God. We loved each other. I felt deep love from hearing and feeling their profound sorrow as they were reminded that life isn't promised.

As I get to spend time with my brothers now, it gets better and better. It's tough to take every time as the last time, but it's not tough to enjoy it. Conversations are more real. The jokes are just as funny. The time is not wasted. To be honest is a gift. Give it. To share your heart is a blessing. Bless someone. It's in being honest with yourself that you can be honest with others and experience true connections. Maybe even the connection of a brother.

Nothing on this earth is more important than the relationships we experience. Strong statement, I know. But what else? Money, success, experiences? Try enjoying those things alone. Relationships enhance everything. Good times are enhanced by others and bad times are less so with company. Life is meant to share. We are made to help each other, challenge each other, and just to be together. I have experienced some amazing things in my short life, but it has been the things I have shared with others that remain the most meaningful and memorable. Some of those times have been on the home field, while others have taken me to far-flung locations around the world.

My first mission trip to Haiti was ultra-special because I shared the experience with "my guys." My Titans teammate Pete Ittersagen and I organized a trip to the northern coast of Haiti. I got my twin younger brothers to come and two of my best friends from Penn State (a former teammate and roommate, Gerald, and a PSU pole vaulter, Matt). I was beyond stoked for the trip. Sure, we would have adventure, but it would be with them! I knew we would laugh and have a good time, but I was most excited about seeing the people I loved serving and experiencing life-changing moments.

The trip did not disappoint. My greatest joy was watching these guys thrive in service. Seeing the Haitian kids flock to my brother Drew (maybe because he bought like fourteen of the name bracelets they made). Watching Gerald—all six-foot seven-inches, and 320 pounds of him—immerse himself in helping at the eye clinic as doctors fixed cataracts and gave people sight. Watching my brother Pete organize the Haitian kids so we could give them pairs of shoes. It was awesome seeing Matt bang on a homemade drum as we played and sang around the old-folks home and various construction sites. Watching my teammates connect with people as they labored to erect a giant military tent to be used as a church on the island of Tortuga. What a great trip! But to experience it with these guys who were special to me enhanced it tenfold. I took pride in my role in helping organize and lead this trip, but more so in bringing this group together.

I could write and write about unique experiences like this that I've had, but the best ones are always with those you love. I hope you have experiences like these and, more importantly, people in your life to experience them with. If not, it must be top priority to build these relationships. I'm so thankful for the relationships I have, but they didn't all happen easily.

I shut myself off from friendships for a while. Life in the NFL will do that to someone, especially when the ground they stand on is as secure as quick sand. I had been cut from the Carolina Panthers after a pretty successful rookie season. I spent three months in football purgatory, with no team to call home and no sense of peace in any city I visited. The Jacksonville Jaguars gave me a job for the end of that season and the off-season, and they used my skills for the preseason before deciding I would be better off on anybody's payroll but theirs. A week later, the Chicago Bears hired me as a hitman, so off I went. My contract in Chicago might as well have been signed on wet toilet paper, because they threatened to flush it more than once. It took them a year to decide my franchise record thirty special teams tackles weren't enough. Though disappointed and baffled by their decision, I was thankful for all that they paid me and the resume builder they were (not to mention the amazing golf I enjoyed in Illinois). The day after being stripped of my Bears jersey, Tennessee called and said I was qualified to wear a Titans uniform.

Can you imagine my confidence level at this point? My sense of job (life) security was about as strong as my application would have been to get into Harvard Law School! In case you lost count, I was fired three times in three years, four teams in four years, four states, four cities, four new sets of people. Just so you know, this is far from uncommon. I have known guys who were on five teams in one year, so I was doing okay with my one-year average turnover rate. You can imagine the difficulty of building relationships under such circumstances. So I just didn't. Well, I fought it as best as I could. I put my head down and went to work. I fought letting my personality show. I didn't want to put myself out there, make a friend, and then be yanked from that location and get hurt again. Best to put up protective shields. This was true at work, but also outside of the facility. I kept it surface with girls I met, knowing with certainty I'd be moving again soon. Of course I hung with the guys and tried to fit in, but I fought letting anybody close. Anybody outside of football was told I moved here for a job. "Where?" they would ask. My answer: downtown. I was great at changing the subject.

All the while, during this span of three or four years, I longed for relationship. For deep connection with people. It's a deeply rooted human need. I fought it as best I could, but nature typically wins. I hesitantly made friends. Some more surface and situational, but others would last a lifetime. There was Alvin Pearman, an NFL journeyman like me. We connected in Jacksonville briefly and then spent a number of years living in Nashville simultaneously as he attended Vanderbilt upon retiring, and I made Nashville home. There's Nick Roach, Chicago starting linebacker and a brainiac Northwestern grad. We had a blast on the field together and challenged each other in our personal lives. I eventually stood in his wedding. He challenged me to think of anybody but myself (we started at once a day), and I challenged him to take his spiritual journey more seriously. There was Thomas Williams, a rookie linebacker I met when I got to Jacksonville. We had breakfast together after being cut the same day. He went off to Seattle and eventually a few other teams, while I set off to the Windy City. We weren't great friends while in Jacksonville, but it was a start. We built a strong friendship years later when my brother moved to California very near where Thomas lived. My visits became more frequent and our friendship grew.

As much as I fought the pain and loss of leaving friends, my need for relationship won. Even struggling-to-make-the-team pro athletes love company. It wasn't that those relationships flourished while I was in my insecure state, but at least I put myself out there to start the foundation of a friendship. I had to be willing to risk losing that relationship if I was moved again, in order to gain the potential for a real connection. And when I did end up leaving, I was always glad to have risked what I did, and it was well worth the risk. I ended up having relationships all over the country because of how transient the football business is.

Alone is lonely. Profound, right? Together is rich.

My journey through the NFL was, for me, the most exciting thing in the world, but to do something like that all alone diminishes the value. This was a major reason my season in Chicago was so special. I played well on the field, but I was able to share it more than any other year with friends and family. Chicago was only four hours from Livonia, Michigan, my hometown, so I was as close as I had been since leaving for college. Mom and dad and hometown friends could easily make the trip. I always had someone at my games that year. Pete was living in Madison, Wisconsin, so he made the two-hour trip to almost every game at Soldier Field. To come and see me play while I was on other teams required a flight and a day off of work, so catching a game or two each year was the most that could be expected. But it was very cool to experience that season in Chicago with so many loved ones there.

Isn't it rewarding to have someone share your successes? Imagine hitting a once-in-a-lifetime hole-in-one on a golf course. As you raise your arms in celebration, you would realize the significance of having friends to share that moment. To have all the wealth in the world, but no one to share it with, is to be poor. The greatest things in life are not things; they are our relationships.

Of course, not all relationships are equal as far as give and take. I have had friendships in which I felt I benefited far more than I could ever contribute. On the flip side, I have also given far more in some friendships than my friend could reciprocate. It is a real joy and pleasure to be able to pour into someone's life even without receiving anything in return, especially when your input leads to growth.

On the other hand, not all relationships are healthy. Each level of friendship has its place as long as proper boundaries are kept. I have had many people who would take far more than I was willing or able to give, draining me when we spent time together, and I have had to limit these friendships because it was not healthy for me. Friends should enhance and encourage one another, not drain and discourage each other. A healthy friendship goes both ways, as both are able to rely on one another when needed. Sometimes you have to make a healthy choice and let a friendship go.

The Look of Friendship

You can only be loved to the extent that you are known. Pastor Pete taught me that. This is a hard truth in friendship. If I choose to only show you one side of me, then that is all you are given to evaluate. You can accept or reject only what you know. If all you know about me is what you have read online, then you might love me, but it's not the same kind of love that comes through a deep experience of who I really am. You only know what you have seen or heard about me, which is only a fraction of who I am. If you know the whole me and then tell me how you feel, well, then I should take stock of what you say. The more of my story that I share with someone, the deeper our friendship can be, as only what is offered up can be open to love or rejection. I'm not saying that all friendships deserve full vulnerability and exposure, but I am saying that being fully vulnerable with a select number of trusted people is most rewarding. To be partially known and loved is an incomplete love, but to be fully known and yet fully loved gives you the sublime joy of being completely accepted as you are.

Chris Redhage, whom I mentioned earlier as a great entrepreneur, having overcome his own obstacles, is one of those friends, someone who knows my strengths and weaknesses, someone I can be open and vulnerable with.

We traveled to Australia twice. The first time we went, it was early in my diagnosis. The second time, however, was at a time when my balance and mobility weren't so great. One day on the trip, we went to the beach and decided to go for a swim.

We started wading in and the waves were pretty high, so to help keep me upright, Chris and I locked arms. And that worked fine getting in the water. After swimming for about a half hour, it was time to get out. Chris and I once again locked arms. The waves were battering me, but I was holding on. Then, a big wave just smashed into us and it spun me around, out of Chris's reach. In recounting the story, Chris tells it this way:

"So here's this 220-pound man being tossed around by the waves. Like an underwater rolling pin. You end up on the beach, face down in the sand. All these people are looking around and wondering what's going on. I knew you were going to be okay, and that I was going to turn you over, and you were going to laugh about it (which you did), and then we were going to get up and keep walking.

"That's what a relationship is. The waves are going to hit, the sand is going to be all over, and it's not going to be pretty. God didn't come down and sit in this pristine castle. We're called to get dirty, to get into this mess. And we're going to keep walking."

That's a friend. Someone to walk with, even if we're unable to walk, ourselves.

Whiteboard Goals: Say It with a Card

Perhaps it's been awhile since you've expressed your appreciation to one of your good friends. If so, now is the time to let that person know you're thankful for the relationship you have. This might also apply to a sibling or a spouse. And guys, it's okay to show a little emotion. If you have trouble expressing your feelings in person, take the Hallmark route: there are plenty of "friendship" cards on the rack that can strike that right tone for you. So pick a card and write a personal note to go with it.

12
Then a Miracle Occurs

There's an old cartoon that shows two scientists standing in front of a chalkboard filled with equations, trying to explain (as I remember it) the Big Bang theory. In the middle of the equations, one of the scientists had written, "Then a miracle occurs." The other scientist points at the board and says, "I think you should be more explicit here in step two."

I wish I could quote cartoonist Sidney Harris and also say about my ALS diagnosis, "Then a miracle occurs." There have been "miraculous" events happening in my life, but they don't include a cure for ALS. I do, however, fight giving in to the disease each and every day.

After a good round of golf (mind you, the tee box gets closer and closer to the green), thinking of the beauty of the course and sharing that time with friends, I lie down at night and ask God—no, I beg God—please don't take this from me.

It's not only beautiful days that evoke this prayer. I cherish even the most difficult ones. For example, just a few days before writing this, I was coming in from my pool. I closed the sliding glass door to the patio and turned to take a step. But my brain was still in its old mode of "thinking" it had full control of my body. I lost my balance and fell backwards. Instead of going down, I tried to recover by backpedaling. Well, I backpedaled right into the upright piano, the force of which twirled me around and bounced me towards the hallway, looking undoubtedly like a human pinball bouncing off furniture. With nothing left to bounce off of, I went down, crashing face-first onto the hardwood floor.

My face and the hardwood were soon covered with blood from gashes to my eye and chin. It's not that they were big gashes, but you know how facial cuts bleed a lot. I ended up with three stitches each in my eyelid and chin. Still, that night when I dropped into bed, my prayer was, "God, it's okay. I don't mind. Just please don't let it get any worse."

Honor Among Titans

But let me tell you about my miracle. It began with a phone call one day, when Coach Mularkey asked me if I would address the Titans team.

He had been on the field at practice two years earlier, when we had done the Ice Bucket Challenge, and I had publicly announced my ALS diagnosis. But after that, he had lost track of me until he saw a video report on my progress.

"We have to get Tim in here," he thought. Three days after he saw the video report, Coach invited me to visit the team at preseason camp.

I brought the players a simple message that day. At the team meeting, I asked the players this question: "What if every NFL locker room was the same? Each locker room had the highly paid running back, the highly drafted quarterback, the big offensive line, and a talented defensive line?" Because the truth is, all NFL locker rooms are like this, full of veterans trying to hang on, guys just comfortable with their positions and contracts, and rookies working to make the team.

Then I asked the guys, "What if the difference between winning and losing was simply how much you cared? What if the team that cared more won? What would it look like to be a team that cared more about each other? What could you accomplish with a locker room full of guys who cared so much that they wouldn't dare not know their playbooks? A team that would work hard, be accountable to each other? A team that cared so much about winning that they did all the right things they needed to do in order to win?"

I went on to ask them to consider that if this was their only shot—and I argued that it was—then they needed to give all they had.

We are called to be our best and do the most with what we have.

"Football is that for you right now," I said. "Be here. Give your all to it."

If they didn't know beforehand that I was a fighter, that I wouldn't give in to ALS, they knew it after my talk.

I said to the team, "I look at myself in the mirror and say, 'Screw you, ALS. You can't have me. Today, I will give my best.' And if you care enough to give your best every day, you will find the success you want."

Coach Mularkey told me he had many coaches who have been in the league twenty or thirty years come up to him and say they had never heard somebody speak like that and deliver a message that touched everyone in the room. After the talk, Coach told me that he FaceTimed his wife and she asked him, "Are you crying?" He admitted he was tearing up because he was so moved by my words to the team.

I don't tell you this to build myself up as this great public speaker or anything. That's not the point. And you have to remember, thanks to ALS, I now speak with a slur. Words no longer come out of my mouth crisp and clear. In fact, sometimes you have to really listen to catch what I'm saying.

My point is that the message rings true.

It's about caring, whether that's through supporting mission work with a local church, respecting your employees, mentoring the next generation, or helping others find success. It's about being prepared. Controlling what you can. It's about pursuing your passion.

Of course, I was grateful for the opportunity to speak with the team. I had enjoyed being with the players, talking shop, thinking about those Sunday afternoon games. Because of my career—as someone fighting for a spot on a team, as a captain and special teams ace, and as a guy striving for game time as a linebacker—I could relate to just about everybody.

Talking to the guys that day reminded of my first official start in the NFL. I knew what it was like to fight for not only game time, but for the role of starter. You would think that after playing three seasons in the NFL, I would have gotten some good time on the field as a linebacker. I mean, I'd actually dressed and played in thirty-two games and made forty-seven tackles through three full seasons in the league. But I had never played a single down of real defense during anything other than a preseason game! I had been close, even put on notice if a certain defensive package was called, or if this guy went down I would get in, but it just never happened.

I had started my fourth season, for my fourth team, the Tennessee Titans. I didn't arrive in Nashville until late Sunday night of week one of the season—I was cut by the Bears on Saturday and claimed off of waivers by the Titans on Sunday. Knowing that I would dress and play special teams right away, Dave McGinnis, the linebackers coach, took me out to walk through some defenses in case I'd have to play in an emergency situation. I could already tell he was a good coach and a good guy. I knew nothing about the Titans defense at this point, so Coach McGinnis just went through the basics.

The Titans had some unique situations going on at the linebacker position. They had a veteran, David Thornton, who had been a long-time star and was coming off of hip surgery. The coaches were keeping him on the PUP (physically unable to perform) list, which meant they didn't have to count him on the roster for at least six weeks. They also had a rookie who had played substandard football so far, so they didn't trust him to dress and play on game day. There was also a second-year starter who had been suspended four games for testing positive for performance enhancers. This led them to pick me and another linebacker, Pat Bailey, off of waivers. Pat and I would become roommates and go on to dominate on special teams and become good friends.

I saw no action on defense through the first seven games, but I came close a few times. By then, I knew the defense well enough and had earned the coaches' respect, so when the opportunity came I knew I'd get my chance. We'd had a couple linebackers get injured who were out for the season, and I knew I was the next man up. Our three starters were healthy going into week eight against San Diego, and I was in for our "heavy" package, which was our short yardage or goal line package, where we play an extra linebacker and take out a defensive back. I practiced at this spot all week, along with my regular duties, knowing very well that I could get in the game on defense. I told only a few people about my role, but made sure to not make a big deal out of it, because who knew if I would actually get in? We were playing at San Diego, so my mom and my brother Steve had flown out to visit brother Drew in Los Angeles. They, along with Drew's wife, Erica, made their way to the game.

We kicked off to open the game, and I jogged off the field as the defense came on. I wasn't even to the sideline yet when I heard our guys shouting out, "Heavy! Heavy!" I immediately changed directions without even thinking and headed to the huddle, giving the personnel signal as I ran in. I knew I might go in, but on the first play? "Extra Backer Zone Screw" was called in the huddle, and I took my alignment. San Diego ran a power play away from me so I flowed, following the ball. But then, the ball carrier cut back towards me. I stepped up and met him along with another defender and stopped him for a short gain. A tackle on my first play!

The next call was for our base defense, so I came out and it was over. Not a person in the stadium was concerned or aware of the significance of that moment for me, except for my four-person cheering section in the upper deck somewhere. I went on to make two more tackles on defense in the game, even one play for a loss, and played ten snaps or so on defense. It really was no big deal, and I really felt that way. I felt comfortable out there. It confirmed what I had felt my whole career. All I needed was an opportunity.

We lost the game, but as I headed for the bus, my teammate David Thornton walked beside me.

"Hey bra, nice job." I thought he was talking about playing defense, because he knew I had never gotten any time before. He went on, "Bro, you got the GS! That's huge!"

"What do you mean?" I asked.

"On the stat sheet, you got that GS!"

I was still trying to figure out what in the world he was talking about.

"You were out there for the first defensive play, so you got an official Game Start. That's huge."

Not only did I get my first plays on defense, I got my first official start!

I saw my family after the game, and they knew the significance of what had happened and shared in my small victory. Maybe, like me, they had been waiting for that to happen. All the hard work, all the lessons I had learned along the way were paying off!

A Titan for Life

After I'd given my speech and had finished mixing it up with the team, I figured I'd be back to my daily life away from the game. What I didn't know was that General Manager Jon Robinson and Coach Mularkey had gotten together after my talk and had a different idea.

Coach had always said in the past that it's really important for him to teach players not just about football, but about how to be better men, better husbands, better dads, better people. He believed that I could have an impact on the players' lives, not just in the building, but outside the building as well.

"We need to sign Tim," Jon Robinson told Coach. "We need to sign him right now."

A player had just been cut and there was one roster spot open. That spot, they decided, would go to me.

I was thrilled to receive the news. The contract would be for one day. After that, I would be put on the reserve/retired list.

In other words, this meant I would be a Tennessee Titan for life.

How cool was that? And the way it was announced to the team was a great deal of fun. During a team meeting, while I was out of sight in the hallway, Coach told the team that they were bringing in a linebacker and a special teams ace to fill the final open roster spot. Then Jon Robinson swung open the door and I walked in, followed by my parents and my brother and his wife. The team jumped to their feet and cheered and gave me fist bumps as I walked down the aisle to the front of the room.

It was an incredible moment. I was now the only player in NFL history to hold an active roster spot after an ALS diagnosis.

In addition to expressing my appreciation, I made sure to point out to everyone that with a contract came a signing bonus, and I looked toward Coach and Jon, wondering where it was. That, of course, got a laugh from the guys.

The big part of my message to the team on that special day, the biggest part of my message to you right this moment, begins with the simple truth that should motivate you to blitz life: all you have is now.

That room full of athletes only needed to look at me to see a living example of that truth.

The Mop's a Prop

Even though my story may carry meaning for others, it doesn't mean I don't have difficulty dealing with a terminal disease. For me, it's not the death part that I don't want to deal with. I don't want to deal with the process of getting there.

I have needed—and still need—help, so I've sought help and support from a counselor named Stephen James. He helps me to live true to myself through this awful sickness, and it turns out that my hour spent exploring thoughts and feelings with Stephen is usually my favorite hour of the week.

Stephen, in our counseling sessions, talks about embracing difficulty and struggle—we all experience it. From that pain comes courage and passion. "Other than athletes, Navy Seals know this," Stephen said during one of our sessions. In order to make it through the pain, the adversity, we have to have something greater than the pain. In my mind, that means we have to have a passion for something worthwhile.

Stephen said we must ask ourselves this question: "What am I willing to lose at? What's worth having my heart broken over? That doesn't have to be extraordinary," he said. "You could be made to go fly fishing, if that's what you're made to do. Some people are made to draw." He also pointed out you can have a passion without getting paid for it.

I can't help thinking about this remarkable man I saw profiled on the local news. His name is Freddie Wiggins, and he's been working as a janitor at St. Thomas Hospital for thirty-six years. As he mops the hallway floors, he gives out warm greetings, calling the not-so-young visitors and patients "young lady" or "young man." They smile and say they haven't been called that in a while. A nurse said he's full of positivity and just picks up everyone's mood.

"I make them happy; they make me happy," he said.

The reporter explained it's "his way to soothe patients and visitors on their cloudy day. The mop is just a prop."[1]

His job may be janitor, but he was made to bring light into people's lives. There's a certain humility and wisdom in this gentleman, something we can all learn from.

One of the great insights I've learned by talking with Stephen—and something I brought up early in the book—is that our job is not who we are.

Neither is a disease.

I am not just a football player.

I am not defined by ALS.

You are more than what you do. In fact, Stephen said understanding who we are starts with a vibrant relationship with God.

"We are created by love, for love, in love," he said. And that works for people of every culture and religion. People that recognize there is a Being greater than themselves do better than someone with the view that we're merely highly evolved mammals.

You'll notice that just about every person that I used as examples of passionate, impactful people, all made explicit statements about their *spirituality*. I didn't set out purposely to make this a "spiritual" book about success, but the truth is that God is naturally a part of who I am. I guess it's not surprising that I became friends with people who try and seek a daily relationship with God, too.

And just look at their life journeys!

It's remarkable that so many of them not only share a spiritual element, but other meaningful traits as well. They are all mission-oriented, accepting of others, highly ethical, spontaneous in thought and action, BS detectors, appreciative of life experiences, empathetic, compassionate, and creative. Finally, they have all had "mountaintop" experiences— moments of overpowering emotion or exaltation, awe, and wonder—which carry over to their everyday lives. All these traits belong to people who are, according to psychologist Abraham Maslow, "self-actualized."[2] Self-actualized just means that they are on a path of growth and development, becoming who they *want* to be in life and reaching their full potential.

You don't have to be perfect to be self-actualized, and you don't have to have all of the above traits. Self-actualization is about moving in the right direction. But I don't think it's a coincidence that the people I've talked about not only have these traits, but are also successful. I think the stories of people like Chris Redhage, Morris Chapman, Britnie Turner, Marcus Cobb, Melinda Doolittle, and Mike Brody-Waite, to name a few, provide real-life examples of what it looks like to actually live on that path to becoming the best they can be.

Back to the Whiteboard

As I began life after football and after receiving the ALS diagnosis, I wrote as one of my whiteboard goals that I wanted to "impact others." But never would I have dreamt that I could once again have an impact on NFL players.

The remarkable new chapter of my journey is that the Tennessee Titans have fully embraced me as part of their team. I go to some practices and games and even travel with the team. I even get the chance to assist the special teams with scouting and film study. It's been so good for me to be back in that team environment, and I believe it has been good for them to have me around.

The other day, when I was visiting the Titans practice field, one of the quarterbacks came up to me and said, "Ever since you spoke to the team, I write your name at the top of my notebook every morning."

To hear something like that is a humbling experience. To be part of challenging and inspiring people is a huge blessing. I'm glad something good can come from my battle with ALS. And as you have read over these pages, you've seen that it's a fierce battle, one that I won't give up on.

In fact, just the other day I replaced my whiteboard goals with new ones:

- WALK

- TALK

- THRIVE

I believe we know when our goals need to change. Something happens. A chain of events or a shift in mindset. For me, walking and talking have become more difficult, so I've needed new goals. Simple as that.

Given the history of ALS, I understand that there are no survivors. But I am holding on and holding out for as long as I can—for a medical breakthrough or a miracle. In the meantime, while I battle this disease, I not only want you to pursue, I want you to *blitz* your life.

Run at it with all you have.

Run full speed.

Don't waste any more time.

If you haven't yet written down your goals, your passion, and your dreams, do it *now*. And I want to hear *your* stories. Next year. In two years. In ten years.

No, I'm not dying. I'm living! And I am going to keep on blitzing life.

ACKNOWLEDGMENTS

I always thought I would write a book, but thinking and doing are not one and the same (if you don't know that by now, go back and read this book again!). Thanks to those of you who encouraged me to share my story. Thanks to Annie Downs for so under-confidently saying that since she wrote books, then of course I could. Thanks, Grace, for trekking from down under to turn my writing into identifiable English (and for crashing my truck while doing so). Thanks, Greg Daniel, for believing we would get this professionally published and setting me on the right path.

Thanks, Richard, for embracing your crazy as you translated mine into words that would impact and inspire. Thanks, Matt West (the newest sports-book guy), for bringing this to the finish line like only a wild sprinting linebacker could. And thanks to the Tennessee Titans organization for supporting my every move.

All of you—your belief in me allowed me to believe even more in myself.

NOTES

ONE: CRAZY LOVE
1. Morris Chapman, *I Know the Plans* (Spring Hill, TN: Cool River Pub, 2013).
2. "Goals Research Summary," Dominican.edu, http://www.dominican.edu/academics/ahss/undergraduate-programs/psych/faculty/assets-gail-matthews/researchsummary2.pdf.

THREE: A SHOE OF A DIFFERENT COLOR
1. Robert Fulghum, *Uh-Oh* (New York: Ballantine Books, 1993).
2. Melinda Doolittle, *Beyond Me: Finding your Way to the Next Level*, (Grand Rapids, MI: Zondervan, 2010).
3. Malcolm Gladwell, *The Tipping Point* (Boston: Little, Brown and Company, 2000).

FOUR: BLITZ YOUR PASSION
1. "Football manager gives behind-the-scenes look at Penn State football," Penn State News, July 31, 2007, http://news.psu.edu/story/194793/2007/07/31/football-manager-gives-behind-scenes-look-penn-state-football.
2. Ibid.
3. Ryan Jones, "Spider Caldwell, Back Where He Belongs," *The Football Letter Blog*, January 21, 2015, https://thefootballletter.com/2015/01/21/spider-caldwell-back-where-he-belongs/.

SIX: THE EASY ROAD
1. "Ronnie Coleman: Evabudy want ta be uh bodybuilda...," YouTube video, 3:26, posted by Scotty Steiner, October 26, 2011, https://www.youtube.com/watch?v=x1AjtX3C5j8.

SEVEN: SLAP ME UPSIDE THE HEAD
1. *Wikipedia*, s.v. "Arnold Schwarzenegger," last modified December 1, 2016, https://en.wikipedia.org/wiki/Arnold_Schwarzenegger.
2. Jessica Bliss, "Maplewood chess team: From novices to state tourney in a year," *The Tennessean*, March 25, 2016, http://www.tennessean.com/story/life/2016/03/24/dark-horse-maplewood-team-chess-much-more-than-game/82094556/.
3. Lee Jussim, "Teacher Expectations," Education.com, December 23, 2009, http://www.education.com/reference/article/teacher-expectations/#A.
4. "Whether You Believe You Can Do a Thing or Not, You Are Right," Quote Investigator, February 3, 2015, http://quoteinvestigator.com/2015/02/03/you-can/.

ELEVEN: GOOD INVESTMENTS
1. http://www.pnas.org/content/107/38/16489.full
2. http://www.payscale.com/career-news/2011/10/the-one-percent

TWELVE: THEN A MIRACLE OCCURS
1. http://www.wsmv.com/story/32232523/st-thomas-janitor-brings-sunshine-to-hospital
2. http://www.simplypsychology.org/maslow.html

ABOUT THE AUTHORS

Tim Shaw

As linebacker and Special Teams Captain for the Tennessee Titans, Tim Shaw was known for his speed, hard-hitting ability, and enthusiastic leadership skills. His seven years in the NFL included seasons with the Carolina Panthers, Jacksonville Jaguars, and the Chicago Bears, where he set a club record for special teams tackles. He was also named to the USA Today All-Joe Team, honoring the NFL's unsung and underrated players. As a three-year starter and graduate of Penn State, Tim earned Academic All-American honors. He also holds an MBA from George Washington University. Now an entrepreneur and investor, Tim is a frequent motivational speaker and supporter of ALS awareness. Blitz Your Life is his first book.

You can follow Tim on Facebook at www.facebook.com/TShawsTruth or Twitter at @TShawsTruth. To learn more about how you can support the fight against ALS, go to ALSA.org.

Richard Sowienski

Richard Sowienski is associate professor at Belmont University and directs the first undergraduate Publishing Program in the U.S. He's held a variety of writing, marketing, editorial, and consulting jobs for publishing start-ups and national magazines, including Better Homes & Gardens, Raising Teens, Country America, Successful Farming, and The Missouri Review. He and his wife Rola cofounded and own a coffee shop in a wooden-shoe factory, so when Richard's not teaching or working on his novel—set in a wooden-shoe factory, naturally—you'll find him savoring light roasts at his favorite Nashville spots.